# Bi-Polar on Benefits

## I Can't Be the Only One

## *Sandy Knox*

**chipmunkapublishing**
the mental health publisher
empowering people with bi-polar affective disorder

Sandy Knox

All rights reserved, no part of this publication may be reproduced by any means, electronic, mechanical photocopying, documentary, film or in any other format without prior written permission of the publisher.

> Published by
> Chipmunkapublishing
> PO Box 6872
> Brentwood
> Essex CM13 1ZT
> United Kingdom

**http://www.chipmunkapublishing.com**

Copyright © Sandy Knox 2009

Foreword by Cara Aiken

Chipmunkapublishing gratefully acknowledge the support of Arts Council England.

**Bi-Polar on Benefits**

**Me Mam and Dad**

Sandy Knox

# Bi-Polar on Benefits

## Contents

Foreword by Cara Aiken

Introduction

| | |
|---|---|
| Chapter 1: | The Beast Itself |
| Chapter 2: | My Beast |
| Chapter 3: | Medical Experience |
| Chapter 4: | Social Care Experience |
| Chapter 5: | Quality of Life |
| Chapter 6: | A Word with the Government |
| Chapter 7: | Head-Hunters Pick Us! |
| Chapter 8: | Self-Help Books & the Like |
| Chapter 9: | Relationships |
| Chapter 10: | What Next? |

Sandy Knox

# Bi-Polar on Benefits

## Foreword

My earliest memory of Sandy is of a very quiet, pretty, blonde, sad girl wandering through the gardens of Sutton Manor Clinic with two watering cans! We were both patients at the same psychiatric hospital in a quaint, old manor house set in beautiful, though neglected grounds. Sandy appeared to be an introverted and shy person and was clearly suffering from the enormous pain and torment that go hand in hand with mental illness.

My life too had come crashing down around me since a recent diagnosis of Bi-polar Disorder. In fact, my life had crashed head on some years before with the onset of Post Natal Depression – my first true experience of mental torture, which lead me to write and publish a book on Post Natal Depression.

On seeing Sandy for the first time, I decided she was to become my friend, but despite my determination to befriend her, she seemed 'unreachable'. A lost soul in a huge world. But, with my 'balls' still intact, I gradually and gently broke through her defences!

Our lives seemed to be running parallel. We had both enjoyed good careers, lovely homes, children we loved, security and family support and then we lost everything and at the same time – our homes, our marriage, our family. It became a fight or flight situation. With enormous, but 'wobbly' strength and determination we chose to fight.

Sandy had been diagnosed, by a private psychiatrist, as having Bi-polar Affective Disorder, though, as she says in her book, it took an extremely long time for the NHS to acknowledge her illness. She went through hell during these years. Her book offers the reader an honest account of the major hurdles she endured over these years, fighting for a diagnosis from the NHS and defending herself from the DSS when, as she says in her book, they allowed her to 'slip through their net' leaving her with no sustainable income to support herself and her son, sometimes for months on end. She had to fight with, sadly, ever-failing strength over and over again.

It was said to me by a friend, "you're so lucky not to have to work". She then went on to say "I might go to my doctor pretending to be depressed and get Benefits so I don't have to work – it would be easy to do and it would give me a much needed rest from working"! This was obviously her perception of me. It hurts me deeply that anyone would think I 'choose' to "live off the Government" and for anyone out there with this warped perception, I would beg them to read Sandy's account of the struggles, the shattered hopes and the deflation of "living off the government" due to mental illness. I hope it is clear to every reader that we also bear the pain of lost pride and dignity as well as the pain of illness.

## Bi-Polar on Benefits

Above everything, Sandy still has her Geordie sense of humour and together we try to laugh at ourselves – when manic in particular! We try to focus on and remember the funny things, not wallow in bad memories. Sandy is the only friend who understands the tiny achievements I make – I remember telling her one day that I had actually moved my washing basket from one room to another and she gave me so much praise!

I have always recognised Sandy's flair for writing and her creative skills, even if she hasn't! Today, as I sit here and write this Foreword, I feel honoured. Sandy may have been through the mill more times than she'd care to remember, but her creativity, intelligence and huge heart still shine through like the brightest star in the sky.

Sandy's and my lives are running parallel still. As she completes this book I am completing my second book, on the subject of Bi-polar Disorder and families.

By Cara Aiken
Author

Sandy Knox

# Bi-Polar on Benefits

## Introduction

There's only one set of footprints in the sand and I ain't on nobody's back!

If you are new to manic depression I wouldn't advise you read this. This is for those who have had eons of the damn thing. Those who now find themselves saying "heard it!" to any bearers of advice. This is a book about the reality of living with Bi-polar when you've got nothing, lost everything. The diversity between say, Bi-polar on Benefits and Bi-polar on Bollinger!

As I impart my take on living with depression and mania in today's world when you're in debt, unemployable and at the mercy of the NHS and DSS, I hope to illustrate the mind-numbing, 24/7 grind of hauling yourself through life, as if life wasn't hard enough. Debts, frustration, tedium, worry are just typical feelings of everyday people about everyday life, then add depression and its accomplices, self-loathing, loneliness, terror, hopelessness, panic, shame. I struggle with consistently low and often severe bouts of paralysing depression, anxiety and/or panic interlaced with very welcome but brief periods of pleasant normality and, if the Gods are favourable, just a mild mania.

You think just like everyone else does about your recent depression, inverted commas, that you were pathetic and weak and you should have pulled yourself together. And their opinion of me when I'm manic and over-the-top? They probably think I'm silly, which is a name-tag that has me cringing with shame. Even in well times the self-loathing remains, simmering away, searing you now and again when you least expect it.

I didn't imagine my recovery would be taking quite so long and really it shouldn't be, but there have been traumas along the way and, of course, problems with the NHS and DSS (aka Jobcentreplus), who have repeatedly failed me and consequently made things worse to the point of unbearable and unbearable is a dangerous state to be in. Based on the law of averages alone, I can't be the only one experiencing such problems, I can't be.

# Bi-Polar on Benefits

## Chapter 1: The Beast Itself

One minute I'm Jane Eyre, flat-irons in hand, trudging round a rainy yard and the next I'm leading a street carnival in sequins and not much else!

I have Manic Depression. The modern term for it is Bi-polar Affective Disorder. Getting rid of the word manic (sounds too much like the word maniac) is an improvement. On the other hand Bi-polar, having nothing to do with bears, sexuality or global warming is a fair description as one's mood does slide up and down on an axis between two extremes.

I'm at one end of the pole or the other. On top of the world, over-confident and impulsive or under a stone, justifying my existence, terrified and aching to die. I spend very little time lolling around on the equator, sadly. The aim is, of course, to achieve the happy medium, whatever that may be, which is what the medication is intended to help me do.

Bi-polar Disorder is a chemical imbalance. If the brain were an engine, then it is mis-firing, can't get the timing right, a bit dodgy and, guess what, there's no customer service department. Sometimes the imbalance sends me into party mood (which doesn't always go down well during the day) and sometimes, most often, it sends me into the realms of despair.

It's a bespoke illness. Everyone's depressions and manias are unique, even though we share the same symptoms we experience them differently, at different times, for different reasons, in different combinations and at different levels. Although some of us have a fair idea, no one really understands what you're going through except you.

**Hypomania**

This is the Aston Martin of mindsets in my opinion. Your engine is running with precision timing, high power output, low maintenance, great MPG! On the scale, hypomania sits on the cusp of mania. Happiness, joy, calm, creativity, energy, stamina, drive and contentment buzz away just a tad above normal without any negative, destructive thoughts or feelings. Oh, to be hypomanic.

**Mixed Episode**

A mixed episode is when mania and depression run at the same time, in simple terms, up and down, happy and sad at the same time. Doesn't seem possible, I know. For me it's being hopelessly depressed, scared, and unable to move whilst at the same time feeling hot with excitement, passion and enthusiasm; it's like having your arms tied down when you're revving with energy and raring to go. A Lada with a Lamborghini engine. The overall effect is sheer physical and mental frustration. I can be agitated, pace the floor. I can't rest, but I want to. I fight and argue with myself. Half of me is demanding that I get on and do something fantastic with my boundless energy whilst the other half is begging, pleading to be left alone. What do you do? What can you do? Always it ends in an exhausted depression.

## Rapid Cycling

Rapid-cycling is when one's mood fluctuates between both ends of the pole within a short space of time; there may be no set pattern. A diagnosis of rapid cycling is reached if the patient experiences four episodes per year. The moods can be extreme or they can be mild. If I experience only four episodes per month I consider myself lucky!

## Ultradian Cycling

This is when one's mood fluctuates weekly, daily, even hourly between mania and depression; for me it usually involves mixed episodes as well. Even a simple exercise can become a devastating disappointment. For example, I might embark on a project, full of creative energy, focus and excitement. For me it's usually something art or craft related which means getting all the materials and equipment together and preparing a workspace. I enjoy my creative highs, but they never last long because my mood will drop, I will slip helplessly down the pole. As always I'm left staring at the aftermath, unable to fathom why I wanted to paint plates in the first place or what I could possibly find enjoyable in the chaos covering my table. If I'm lucky, I won't have spent any money. It's impossible to function and the longer it goes on the deeper the resulting depression. The pain of failure adds self-loathing to the equation and deepens the subsequent depression.

## Clinical Depression

A clinical depression is a depression that's serious enough to require specialist medical treatment as opposed to depression which the mind can and will heal by itself, perhaps with the help of a GP.

## Physical Effects

It's not just my mood and my thinking mind that are affected by the extremes of Bi-polar. The body, in fact, everything about me is affected. My muscles, when depressed, are heavy and slow to move. My energy levels are low. My thinking is slow. My senses of smell and taste are dulled, hunger pains halted, my eyes won't focus and blinking has to be done manually. All the body's functions are depressed. The body's need to recharge, recover, to sleep, is paramount.

In mania my body is able to command consistently high energy levels on very little food, though the food I do have time to eat is consumed with passion and greatly enjoyed. I feel light on my feet,

## Bi-Polar on Benefits

my muscles are strong and joints flexible. I notice detail in everything with renewed focus. My thoughts are clear and organised. The body's need to burn excess energy, to do stuff, is paramount.

### Triggers

Anything that causes a shift in mood is a trigger. In other words, a stressful experience (good or bad) can be the trigger for an onset of mania or depression and the associated fear, etc that could go with it.

### Giving Birth to the Beast

Childbirth can trigger depression, mild, moderate or severe which is known as Post-Natal Depression (PND). It happens because the new mother's hormones have not returned to normal activity. There is a hormonal imbalance. Bi-polar Disorder is a hormonal illness and childbirth can trigger it too.

For the record Bi-polar is a hereditary illness, but that doesn't mean it will be passed-on, it means there is a possibility that it could. I will not pretend to know anything on the subject of post-natal onset of Bi-polar or PND, but there are many good, reliable resources of information and contacts available to us, the NHS Direct website being a good place to start.

## Fear, Anxiety, Stress, Paranoia, the Whole Works

Depression takes over. It moves in with all its baggage, sets up home and refuses to budge. It won't allow me to do anything. I'm a hostage and I don't know what it wants or what its terms are. I don't know when I'll be released. I don't know if I'll be fed, allowed to sleep or terrorised. I will let people down. No one will understand. Thus, fear, anxiety, stress, paranoia, the whole works.

## Suicide

Coward is the name I've heard used to describe those who've committed or have attempted suicide. Nice.

Considering no one knows what awaits us after death, I think it's brave to leave the world you know for one you don't. Alone. For me death is an end to the torture and, if I'm lucky, a place of peace.

> *The thought of suicide is a great source of comfort: with it a calm passage is to be made across many a bad night.*
>
> *Friedrich Nietzsche*

Manic Depression, or Bi-polar Disorder, is a serious, life-threatening illness. Statistics reveal that one in seven will end their suffering for good. That's pretty serious. God bless them.

## Crisis Teams

Crisis Teams are there for those in mental crisis, the clinically ill who are experiencing suicidal feelings. The crisis team removes the need for hospitalisation. The severely clinically depressed, that is those who have attempted suicide and those whom doctors daren't trust not to kill themselves, need hospital care. In hospital a patient can be kept safe, be monitored at 15, 20 or so minutes intervals, medicated and fed in a no stress environment (as bleak as no man's land, but there you go).

The Crisis Team may only visit you for a few days or a few weeks depending on how long your crisis lasts. They work alongside, or fluidly, with the CPN (Community Psychiatric Nurse), the community care worker and the treating psychiatrist who can call them in at a moment's notice. It seems to be a very successful set-up and in my experience as an end user, flawless.

## Community Psychiatric Nurses

Fully qualified psychiatric nurses who have hospital ward experience. They ask questions, make notes, listen, support and offer help and advice. In times of crisis the CPN will make regular visits to monitor and observe behaviour and current mindsets, reporting their findings to the psychiatrist. The CPN and the Crisis Team may also attend one or several of the patient's appointments with the treating psychiatrist.

## Care in the Community

I have had excellent experiences of the support provided to me by those who work within the mentally ill community. They're the ones who visit you at home, listen, understand, give you confidence and get you out, if they can. Only lovely people can do these jobs.

## The Medication Trail

There are many anti-depressant, mood stabiliser, anti-psychotic and anti-convulsant drugs and many combinations to try. How they work is a science too complex for me to grasp. The purpose of the anti-depressant is to lift depression using brain-friendly chemicals. Some anti-depressants are also sedative, which can be useful when a depression is shot with panic and nervousness. A mood stabiliser is used to prevent mood-swings. An anti-psychotic can be used to curb mania and negative thinking. Some can be combined. Which one or which combination is right for me or you? Who knows? An anti-depressant prescribed without a mood stabiliser can cause rapid cycling in manic-depressives.

## Bi-Polar on Benefits

Medicines have to be tried until the right one is found and a therapeutic dose achieved. To try only three may take a year. Some cannot be combined and it is necessary to allow a couple of weeks for the old medication to leave the body before a new one can be tried. Even if the first medication is right for you it will take two weeks to a month before it begins to have an effect, if any; two weeks is a long time when you're unwell. Some psychiatrists will see you at intervals of four weeks, sometimes six, two if you're lucky. If your symptoms haven't improved they adjust the dose or change to another medication and you'll leave with an appointment four weeks or so hence and so it goes on.

## Chapter 2: My Beast

I know only one other diagnosed Bi-polar, Cara, a published author on the subject of mental ill-health and by some strange, perverted coincidence we are tied together in very similar boats.  She is out there bravely facing the storm, struggling with the sails, trying to keep on course and I am the coward afraid to leave the relative safety of the harbour. We are just two women whose lives have been razed to the ground.  Two intelligent, caring, strong, decent women, who have lost their confidence, esteem, marriages, careers, respect.  Two women who we're once successful (questionable on my part) now scraping by on Benefits.  A burden on the already overburdened back of society.  Two single mums, scrounging off the taxpayer, who should pull themselves together and get a job!

If only we could.  If only we could get consistent, appropriate medical treatment we would.  And we are asking for it, no matter how many times the NHS and the DSS screws up and knocks us down we'll keep banging on their door, we have no choice.

It's fair to say that depression is the opposite of mania.  I am still the same, recognisable person; it's just that my mindset is different.  In depression I see impossible and in mania I see possible.  The issues that haunt me in depression are considered mere triviailities in mania – just hiccups in the grand scheme of things, so trivial in fact, I brush them off

## Bi-Polar on Benefits

or simply just ignore them... now which credit card should I put this holiday on?

I go with the analogy that my brain is a computer, silly though it sounds. To operate efficiently, all my software has to install successfully every day. As I write this, I can safely say that my writing software did fully install this morning, whereas my "personal appearance" software didn't!

I have divided my mindset into three. I'm depressed, not depressed or manic and there are three levels within each. When I'm depressed, which is most of the time these days, I'm depressed, very depressed or really depressed. And if I'm manic I'm either a bit manic, quite manic or really manic and when I'm neither depressed nor manic I'm usually flat, okay or shell-shocked. That's it.

There is, of course, the fear, anxiety, etc; they also have their own levels.

It's worth bearing in mind though that my 'normal' might be considered depression in someone else. It depends where you were placed on the big mood slide-rule of life. My 'bit manic' might be your happy and equally my 'very depressed' might be your suicide. To go off the scale in depression is, well, to die. To go off the scale in mania, who knows? Mania can be equally life threatening. I might believe I am way more capable of doing something that, in reality, I'm not. For me it could be thinking I have the driving skills of Lewis

Hamilton and kill myself or the business savvy of Sir Richard Branson and risk everything and more on a hunch, who knows!

## My Diagnosis or Lack Thereof

I found out I had Bi-polar Affective Disorder by accident. I self-diagnosed, if you like. About four years ago I read a book, loaned to me by Cara, called 'The Pits and the Pendulums', which made me sit up straight. I related to it in a way that gave me the shivers. So I read a few more books, surfed the net and armed with my notes, my Bi-polar symptoms and a credit card I bought a 30 minute audience with my old private psychiatrist to seek his professional opinion. He diagnosed Bi-polar. It explained a lot.

I am not currently being treated for Bi-polar disorder (nor ever have been) because I have not been diagnosed by an NHS psychiatrist. I have not been diagnosed, I believe, because I have not been seen by one psychiatrist enough times for him to recognise the symptoms. I can recall having seen 16, at least. Some of whom, unbeknownst to me at the time, I would see only once. Where do they go? You have to go over it all yet again. Churn up painful thoughts, feelings and memories with raw, shredded emotions in front of a new psychiatrist, a stranger.

The latest NHS psychiatrist, whom I've seen only two times, isn't treating me for manic depression,

## Bi-Polar on Benefits

but for depression. He's treating me for depression probably because depression's all he's ever seen – all of two times. He will not entertain a Bi-polar diagnosis. In truth I've been in a stable depression when I've seen him, all of two times, or I wouldn't have been able to go! Of course, he can only treat what he sees and what are the chances of a mania coinciding with a 20-minute window every six weeks? He's unlikely ever to see it (unless I become so severely manic that I end up in A&E or the Police Station). So I take the anti-depressants (even though I know they can cause rapid cycling) because maybe they will help; maybe he's right, maybe I am just depressed! Or maybe I'm a hypochondriac, whatever.

What of the diagnosis from the private psychiatrist? Don't know - it is seemingly irrelevant! In my experience psychiatrists rarely concur with another's diagnosis and/or treatment and strangely enough don't seem interested in seeing any medical history notes (so what's the point in writing them then?).

### A Brief Look at the Beginning

There is a lot of interest in Bi-polar at the moment. Celebs stepping up to the podium to share their plight and shed light on a miserable, hopeless illness that can afflict anyone, from any walk of life, at any time. I am so grateful to these people for their openness and honesty. They have helped me, and probably many others, to feel less ashamed.

Since early teens, when depression first introduced itself to me, life has been a struggle. At 15 I was either holed away in my bedroom or glued to the chair every night in front of the telly watching anything and everything until the dot came on. No interest in life. Sad. Depressed. Confused. Scared. Clueless.

I knew by about aged 17 that the likelihood of my succumbing to a major breakdown at some point in my life was great given the amount of times my brain had crashed and re-booted already in its short existence. By my mid-twenties I knew it was inevitable. Looking back I'm filled with sadness for the me that I was, stoically fronting the crashes, secretly and carefully re-installing the infected software, all without anyone knowing. I wish I could go back and give myself some support. All I knew then was that depression was considered a weakness and I was ashamed, so I hid it. It made life very hard and very lonely.

**Preparing for War**

I decided to do something about protecting myself from a breakdown, be a pro-active depressive (I'd not heard of manic depression back then). I read up on subjects relating to positive mental health, spirituality and the like. I even went to see a psychologist for a while but all I got out of that was

## Bi-Polar on Benefits

a complex about being boring! I tried to practise the stuff I believed in and disregarded the rest. I confronted my hang-ups (well worth the effort), analysed myself (frustrating), my childhood (harrowing), everyone around me (tedious) and discovered my core beliefs (relief). I was at the stage where I actually quite liked certain aspects of me. I was centred, grounded, peaceful even and content, sort of (though not necessarily happy). I knew what I believed in and that felt good. Sixteen years of self-study was paying off, though it was a meagre pay-out because in all that time, despite what I'd learned about me, the depressions never failed. They came, they conquered, they went and they came again. Sadness, fear, self-loathing, insecurity and hopelessness floored me every time, shattering my confidence and obliterating any self-esteem.

It's hard to act normally when you're dying inside. It's hard to act happy and interested when you're not; when your brain's shutting down programme by programme right in front of everyone's eyes. I hid it, bottled it up. I coped (at least that's what I wanted people to believe). The self-help, the positive, balanced attitude, though a useful life skill, did nothing to prevent my brain from crashing again and again and it did not prevent a complete breakdown.

## Sandy Knox

**Positive Mental Damage**

Positive mental attitude stuff can be damaging in the wrong hands. A bold statement to make. I pushed my comfort zone, broke through my ceiling and reached for the sky; after all, the worst risk is to take no risk at all, right? If you think successful, you'll be successful. I let myself get caught up in the turbulence of a generation overly keen on high achieving, though I never really succeeded. I tried to love myself, believe in myself and my abilities, but it's not easy when you don't. I spent most of my time either in depression or recovering from the depressions that scuppered almost all of my plans. Dreams and aspirations cast off like excess luggage. Exhausted, hopeless and confused. Wasn't I doing everything right? Shouldn't I be happy now, depression-free? My search for knowledge of self (though helpful in my ongoing recovery today) did little more than encourage me to strive for a life that was much too stressful for me to maintain.

*I've been very depressed for two and a half weeks now. My defences are low. I feel exposed and vulnerable. The pills don't seem to be working now. I'm best on my own, safe in my silent home, just how I like it. I've been very nervous and shaky. I feel fearful, panicky. I can't, won't answer the 'phone or the door.*

*I've been a bit stupid again. I've spent money I haven't got on some ridiculous brilliant idea. I decided it would be a good idea to start up and run*

## Bi-Polar on Benefits

*my own nail business. The equipment I bought, the work, all the practise, the studying, the research. I feel nauseous just thinking about it. And all the people I told, because that's what you do, you tell people and they support you. What must they think of me now? I went on about my business plan, the 'how-to' articles with photos that I would write for magazines. It's embarrassing. And some unbelievably silly idea I had that I could propel myself into the world of high society and fame. I'm mortified, what was I thinking? Yesterday, I decided to just give up the whole business idea. Put it all in a box and try to forget it.*

*The last two and a half weeks since my mood crashed have been a nightmare of depression, anxiety and constant pressure. Pressure to get myself out of the slide before it gained further momentum. Pressure to get back to the way I was three weeks prior when I was motivated, energised, determined and actually enjoying myself with my new passion. But as soon as I came to terms with my decision to forget the whole thing I felt instant relief. The pressure was off. I had mistaken my business idea for a good one. It was a costly mistake, how the hell am I to pay for it?*

**If I'm Depressed**

I want to be quiet. I need peace and solitude. I can get myself to do things, but I have limitations. For example I may not be able to go outside, though I might be able to answer the door or even pick up the 'phone, provided I know who's on the other end and am able to bring up their file in my imaginary computer before the answer-phone kicks in. I may wear make-up, but it will be minimal. I'm fragile. Something feels wrong. There's an atmosphere of doom, not great, not imposing, just there, as a menacing undercurrent. I fear the outside world and the eyes that will judge me. I fear that my eyes will reveal sadness. A clown with a happy paint job!

**If I'm Very Depressed**

My head is in turmoil. Everything is frightening. I sense impending, thundering doom because I can feel it; a heavy, panicky feeling, like the feeling you'd get if you were running for your life in the dark. Like that oppressive pressure you feel just before a big storm. People frighten me.

I'm fighting it; trying to reason with it. But the reality of my situation, the loneliness, the hopelessness, the debt, the fear of the future leaves me in turmoil. I pace. I try to sit. I try the safety of my bed. I wish my bed were in a cupboard. I draw curtains and tilt blinds because I need to be private and, so as not to arouse the neighbours' suspicions that I might still be in bed, I leave them slightly open.

I try to shut myself down, reboot. I cry. I stare, always at the ground. I can feel my heart beating. There's tension in my chest, it hurts. Hour after hour, day after day it doesn't stop. My only goal, my only desire, my only sanctuary is sleep, if I'm lucky.

> *Is this how it's supposed to be?*
> *The dead of night, the moon and me?*
> *Am I so alone?*
> *Show me where the others go.*
> *Let me sleep so I might know.*

## If I'm Really Depressed

My brain is slow, thoughts trickle through my mind, one after the other, but none of it registers or evokes a response; not even my debt problem. I don't care, I can't care, I don't know how. I don't care to answer anyone who speaks to me either, because I can't. I can't get my throat to open up. I'm trying though, I'm really trying, but you don't know that. You think I'm ignoring you, but I'm not, honestly.

Please, I don't think I can do this any more. Please, I just can't, I give up. I know I'm weak, I'm sorry. I should pull myself up, but I can't take any more. I've had enough. Please don't help me. I'm not worth it and I really don't mind.

## Lies

I tell lies and I'd go as far as to say that everyone with a depressive illness tells lies. "Oh, I'm great, hoping to get back to work soon", "I'm just going to lie down, awful headache; too much sun probably",

"I didn't eat all of them", "I had a shower last night", "I intend to send them back", "I'm absolutely fine", "I'm better off on my own", "I always take my medication".

## Mania

*It's a cloudy day with the odd blast of sunlight warming things up here and there. I think it's a beautiful day and I feel fantastic. Those tablets are amazing. I decide to look for a book that I've been nagging myself to read for ages. The book is an account of the life of a Bi-polar sufferer. It was another gift from Cara. Whilst looking for it in a wardrobe I notice my acrylic nails paraphernalia, left over from the attempt at starting up that business. It didn't fail remember, I failed. Again.*

*So I'm sitting here looking at this business in a box and have a brilliant idea. I will restart the business. I'll finish the home-based training course (I'm much too unstable to consistently attend college). I will become a master at acrylic nails and produce exquisite, bejewelled nail art. I will write some 'how to' articles for magazines with step-by-step photos on how to recreate one of my latest, unique designs. I'll use my digital camera. I'll be famous for my works of art, I'll specialise; weddings perhaps. I'll use real diamonds. I'll be nail painting for the glitterati (whoever the hell they are)!*

## Bi-Polar on Benefits

Don't know how long I spent fantasising, I have no concept of time, none whatsoever. My five minutes could have been an hour.

Nevertheless I decided to resume nail training straight away, there and then. I wanted to practise immediately and, with organised swiftness, moved the furniture that blocked clear access to the four boxes. There was no stopping me. Downstairs and unpacked, I organised a workspace on the dining table and started practising.

*I've got everything I need; equipment, materials, tools, ideas, hell I've even got the compressor and air brush, it won't cost me a dime and I can make a lot of money. I'm gonna jump in with both feet, all guns blazing. I'll sell the how-to articles to a variety of magazines and I could even sell a kit for each design, which could be bought from my Website (not that I have one)! I'll contact the papers, they'll be interested in a woman on her uppers who comes up with an ingenious plan to earn a living and get herself off the dole. I know how to play the game, I know that any publicity is good publicity when you're selling something.*

For the second time, I went upstairs, this time to look for a nail magazine and stumbled across the miniature, doll's house-sized room I had built for fun. It has a brick and beam fireplace, flag-stoned floor and skirting boards, even a door. I had made plates, cups, a fire grate, a poker, vessels and vases. I even made loaves of bread in various shapes and sizes, carrots, croissants, sausage rolls, pasties, pies. Then suddenly I had a brilliant idea.

*I'll start a business making and selling miniature creations. Maybe I'll get an outlet for them at the doll's house shop in a nearby town; they won't be able to resist. I will make stunningly realistic, one-off pieces, signed and numbered, of course, for a lot of money. I will do miniature shoes, maybe replicas of the top names like Blahnick and Choo. They will be a must-have for the IT crowd. I'll be famous!*

So, I surfed the net and ordered more materials, as you do. Then, after much thought I decided to run both the nail business and the miniature business together.

*It will make financial sense to do so, two incomes are obviously better than one and I really need the money AND, running two businesses will be of far more interest to the press! It can't fail. I'll get Cara involved, we'll make a fortune.*

## As You'd Expect…

The story's much the same as before, I ordered everything I needed and more, sketched some designs, surfed the net, read the book and then I failed it. And here were the boxes to prove it.

I didn't quite get the 'miniature business' boxes downstairs to the dining table so that I could alternate between the two crafts as and when I felt

## Bi-Polar on Benefits

like it. I got one of the boxes to the landing then noticed the odd sock drawer was stuffed full, so I thought I'd quickly marry up a few pairs, but part way through I came upon a pair of pillowcases I had forgotten about so I changed the bed. I thought I'd wash the dirty bed linen straight away: get them done and back in the cupboard by that night. Really, I wanted to make a cup of tea, relax and get focused on the business ideas that were brimming over in me, but while I was waiting for the kettle to boil, I decided to water the plants, then I noticed the dust. I even took the CDs and DVDs off the shelves so as to clean thoroughly, but half way through, I noticed the unfinished hatch to the kitchen. It wouldn't take long to paint this room, a day, maybe, I thought. So I started estimating measurements which lead to my surfing the net for wooden plantation shutters, which, thankfully, I didn't order. Then for the first time that day I noticed the clock, I had been like a bee in a lavender patch for hours but had achieved nothing. The 'miniatures business' was still in transit at the top of the stairs and the 'nail business' was supposedly operating downstairs. But never mind that.

*I'll make something special for dinner and I'll prepare it now. And while I'm cooking I'll come up with a business name.*

I cooked three different dishes and decided that I would start a parent company so that I could diversify. All my different business ideas would operate under one umbrella. The T-shirt business, the Poo Garden business (don't ask), the water butt that feeds your washing machine business! I didn't get to bed till 4.50am, but I didn't sleep long, too much to do.

Many people, particularly women, will relate to a hectic day of housework and juggling the chores; I'm not expecting sympathy. My point has to be that I may start my day at ten in the morning, but I might still be going at three the following morning, because I can't switch off the creative and physical energy and I don't want to either, it feels too good. I may spend the day innocently dusting my nooks and crannies, reorganising my shoes and re-hanging the curtains but really, more importantly I should be spending that time getting my finances in order, finding a solution to my debt problem, learning to be more thrifty, looking for some sort of income earner, a realistic one and preferably one that can be done at home!

**If I'm A Bit Manic**

If I'm a bit manic I buzz, flitting from one project to another until I have about ten on the go. I sleep little and work solidly, barely stopping to eat. Eating's a chore and I'm much too busy with more important things. I probably haven't got the time or inclination to discuss with you how I'm feeling or what I think of myself, I'm not really bothered, my mind's on other things, maybe later, maybe, if I've got time, okay? My attention can easily be swayed though, and I'll flit from one project to the next until

## Bi-Polar on Benefits

I'm surrounded by chaos. At least, that's what it looks like, but it's organised chaos, I'm totally in control and with my boundless energy and steadfast drive I'll complete everything exactly as planned, eventually, at some point during the episode. However, I am so used to the mood fluctuations that I seem to be able to time my projects to complete before the expected unexpected crash into depression. As if something in my head triggers a reaction that has me automatically winding down, bringing my jobs to a close and tidying things away.

If I'm not experiencing much anxiety, panic or fear then I will be using the 'phone and communicating with the outside world, getting things done, talking to friends and family, maybe. Without these "a bit manic", high-achieving days, my whole world would collapse; they keep me going through the very depressed, non-achieving days. Keep my head above water, so you can all see me waving!

### If I'm Very Manic

If I'm very manic I think I'm the bee's knees. Just all round fab. Everyone else is fab too but not as fab as me. Everyone must want to know me and I'll chat away to anyone really, especially if I think they could really do with it and I'll believe that their lives are infinitely better now for having met me! I'll notice that the birds are really "getting it on" and the startling brightness of colour everywhere is so vivid and bursting with life. I'll feel bathed in a special light as I walk down the street, feeling fab and everyone's looking at me because I'm so fab!

I'll spend hours working on business plans; business plans that evoke surges of excitement as I run clips in my head of my inevitable and imminent success! It will over excite me and I'll struggle for the self-discipline required to suppress a higher mania. I think I'm a genius (undiscovered), which gives me the edge over everyone else! Thank God I only think this. It takes masses of energy to suppress and manage these manias and masses more for the self-discipline not to act on what you believe. I live in fear of the day I make a complete tit of myself!

**If I'm Really Manic**

If I'm really manic I don't bother about how I feel, I don't need to question my self-confidence and ability. "Now if you don't mind, I've got a business to get off the ground. Thank you". There lies the problem. A really manic state could mean complete financial ruin if I leap blindly into a business venture or book a holiday or buy a motorbike! I probably won't listen to you and I definitely won't be taking your advice because I know best. As far as I'm concerned I know what I'm doing, I'm not unwell, I feel better than I've ever felt, I have a sound business idea and a strategy. I'm capable and able and have the energy and determination required to make a success of it.

## Bi-Polar on Benefits

People believe me, so they believe in me. Illness? I'm not going to become ill.

To be honest, I don't necessarily doubt my abilities. I do think I have what it takes to be successful at whatever I choose to do because I know I'll do the work, but I do doubt my ability to maintain the optimum mood, if you like, for longer than a few weeks or months! As soon as my mood crashes, as it always does, the business and all my investment goes by the wayside and I can't always pick it up again – too ashamed, too late and too painful to face the people who believed in me and in my hype.

I have done things which I really should be ashamed of. For example, tarting myself up and going to a nightclub on my own with the sole intention of getting laid! Deciding I would become a sex-line operator and practising! Looking into becoming the first woman of my age as a Page 3 model! Contacting Spearmint Rhino for a job behind the bar! All dangerous situations to be in for a woman who is supremely confident, naive, gullible and trusting that everyone in the world is as wonderful as me.

## Knowing My Limits

I know my limits and I stick to them, or try to. Often I have pushed my comfort zone and it has had flooring results. I have to remember, therefore, to remain within my limits because it's about treating the symptoms. I know what I can and can't do; this means that if I am not able to go out, I don't. If I don't want to talk to anyone or answer the door, I don't. Why push myself? Why make it worse for myself? Why risk deeper depression and all the baggage that comes with it when I know that in a few days or weeks perhaps, I'll be out there strutting my stuff again?

I have set limits for manias, but they're not easy to stick to, especially as I largely ignore them! I have better control when I'm just a bit manic. For example, in a shop full of stuff that, once purchased, would transform the quality of my life, I managed to convince myself that buying pegs in a basket was what would do it, and it did, I got the same buzz, just!

This, to me, is learning to live with it, taking whatever the illness presents on a day-to-day basis and dealing with it according to my mindset. Sometimes I'm okay, sometimes I'm not, c'est la vie!

# Bi-Polar on Benefits

## Chapter 3: Medical Experience

The medical world will tell you that manic depression is very hard to diagnose. I wonder if it has anything to do with the psychiatrist seeing you only once every four weeks for 20 minutes! The likelihood of being able to observe mania and depression is slim because it could take months even years to uncover enough of a pattern in behaviour to be able to give a proper diagnosis, bearing in mind that even a rapid cycler may only have four episodes a year. I could visit the psychiatrist during a manic episode, but there are two reasons that that can't happen; the psychiatrist can't give me an appointment when I need one (you have to wait weeks) and when I'm happy in mania I don't want to see him. I feel fab, why would I need a doctor?

Is a diagnosis of manic depression only accurate on the day it was given? I ask this because the last time I was affected by mania may have been the last time. Who knows? It's also possible that I mistake happiness for mild mania, or vice versa, after all it's been a long time since I knew what happiness felt like without the undercurrent of fear, anxiety and doubt that courses through me. You're either too well to need help or too unwell to care.

Respect to the GPs whom I have always found to be warm and supportive. They seem to understand, after all they're at the front line and see it every day. They are the first port of call and the first to make a diagnosis and will refer you to a specialist when necessary.  They can tell the difference between clinical depression and, let's say, everyday depression, referring the former to the specialists and treating the latter themselves. They listen, they advise, they provide prescriptions and when necessary they can kick-ass and get things moving, as my GP had to do for me concerning the DSS.  They are also known for spending time just talking and listening because they know it helps, a bit like you'd expect a psychiatrist to do!

## Psychiatrists Aren't Head-Shrinkers (Psychologists Are)!

I always assumed, influenced by American television no doubt, that a psychiatrist listens intently whilst you recline on a velvet chaise longue and rattle on about your problems.  Not so.  The psychologist does this but without the chaise.  The psychiatrist is a bit like a GP in that he diagnoses, prescribes drugs, monitors progress and makes referrals, as appropriate, to the relevant specialists within his team for treatment.  In my experience, psychiatrists ask few questions, never tell you what they have diagnosed and never explain anything.  If you ask them to explain they look at you as if you're, well, mad.  He doesn't want to risk getting into serious, often complex discourse with someone who might burst into 'The National Anthem' at any moment, not that I do that, well not that I know of. It's important for me to have things explained.  If I

## Bi-Polar on Benefits

understand what's wrong with me I'm more likely to be able to help myself, it's logical. It is logical, isn't it? Or am I odd? Do only odd people want to discuss the ins and outs of their illness? Is it unhealthy, am I obsessed? Not according to the NHS Direct website.

*"Learn about your illness so that you can recognise the signs of an approaching episode, and can take the necessary steps to manage it successfully."*

*Taken from NHS Direct Website's Health Encyclopaedia under Bipolar Disorder.*

### The Private Path

If you're fortunate enough to have a whole pot of money or health insurance, you can tread the private route, though you could end up on thin ice with your insurer. With an enduring illness like manic depression, you can't blame them if they get uneasy about the money you and your never ending "illness" are siphoning from their coffers and start looking for clauses in their small-print (else start writing new ones) to get rid of you. I doubt I'll get private health cover ever again, if I could afford it, but I could be wrong.

The private psychiatrist has all the mental health tools in the known world to help you provided you can come up with the money. Hospitals, psychiatric clinics and retreats, medications not available on the NHS, counsellors, therapists, psychologists, Neuro Linguistic Programming (NLP) and Cognitive Behavioural Therapy (CBT) practitioners, you name it money can buy it. The medication trail is still the same, but you may try different drugs for shorter periods of time because the private psychiatrist will see you more often in order to monitor your response more closely. The NHS psychiatrist can't afford to see you as often as he'd like, but the private psychiatrist can see you as often as you can afford. Not that I think you should rush to make another appointment.

The private specialist (£100 a half-hour back in 2003) didn't want to explain much either it seemed. They will if you press. One psychiatrist I saw was unable to find much to say to me so spent most of the half hour talking about himself and what he hoped to accomplish in his bright, achievable future, even over-running the appointment on a couple of occasions in order to conclude.

## John With the Purple Hands

There was an old man on my ward named John. He was in his seventies; I sketched him on a scrap of paper. He was thin, pale, gaunt and his clothes just hung from him. He never spoke, ever. A few times I sat with him and held his hand. I got a tiny response. He would often wander the circular corridors endlessly or stand motionless, arms and head hanging.

## Bi-Polar on Benefits

One day he stood in the corridor for nearly four hours completely motionless. That's a long, long time. His face was pale, bloodless yet his hands were purple. I went to get the nurse who looked at him and said "oh don't worry, he's always doing that" and went back to her station. He stood there for over eight hours, his face pale grey and his hands a deep purple-red, as if the blood in him had stopped circulating.

No one spoke to him. There was no one to speak to him. No one cared. All I know about him was that his wife had died and his heart had broken. This was the year 2000, the 21$^{st}$ century, the new Millennium!

NHS hospitals are still bad if Cara's recent experience counts. She had to be admitted to Harlow Psychiatric ward just before Christmas 2006 because her new psychiatrist, third one in six months, had over-prescribed Carbamazapine. She was told to take 1000mg though Cara had repeatedly explained that she had reacted badly on 800mg. But what does Cara know? So Cara was over-dosed, became seriously unwell and had to be admitted to hospital to be detoxed. The experience deepened her depression and brought with it suicidal feelings. In hospital she was to be observed every 15 minutes by a member of the nursing team. A male patient, shortly after he'd had a violent outburst on the ward, came into her room, stood at her bedside and stared at her for 25 minutes. No one came. She was terrified. She managed, somehow, to hide the severity of her symptoms and get herself discharged. Respect.

You have to have your wits about you on a psychiatric ward! You know nothing of the patients you are forced to live with on a locked ward with unlockable bedrooms. You don't know why the other patients are there and under what circumstances and apart from the danger element you don't want to risk the embarrassment of any 'National Anthem' renditioners! Unfortunately, you're in there in the first place because you haven't got any wits, so to speak! What do you do?

**Continuity is Key**

The first major problem for me has been the lack of continuity. I would see a psychiatrist at my local mental health centre (a place where psychiatrists see their patients and social workers and care in the community are organised), I'd go back for my next visit and there'd be a different one, next visit a different one again. And the new ones don't seem to care what has gone before; they do their own thing. Start you afresh on a new medication and tell you to come back in a month. We're not dealing with a persistent cough here; we're talking life-threatening illness.

When I was admitted to hospital the first time, I responded to a Dr E (who had a glowing reputation), but she left and, apparently, I stopped responding. Continuity and trust are vital.

# Bi-Polar on Benefits

## My Intention is Not to Offend, But…

Call me racist if you damn-well dare, but I have a problem with some of the foreign accents - I can't always understand what they're saying and there are some very big words in psychiatry! Just a few communication lessons is all that's needed here, the kind you'd offer anyone who relies on communication with other people to get their job done.

There was one doctor whom I eventually couldn't see any more because I couldn't understand what he was saying to me. I never doubted his ability and he was professional, as are most of the psychiatrists I've seen, but he would become frustrated with me because he had to repeat himself so many times. I felt awful about it and would be filled with anxiety prior to the visits (what's new there?) so in the end I said, for one reason or another, that I couldn't see him anymore. That doesn't go down well on file, I bet.

Cara's general opinion of psychiatrists is much like mine. We both agree that pre-breakdown, before we'd met, we found psychiatrists a bit scary. Simply put, if we met one at a party, we'd avoid them like the plague for fear of being analysed by an obviously perfect being. Now, we're not afraid of them at all, in fact we even have the guts to confront them if need be, not that it does any good! They're just normal people like you and me with hang-ups and baggage, secrets, failings, flaws and personality problems!

## Am I Really That Boring?

I saw an NHS psychologist for a short while, many years ago. He looked remarkably like Danny De Vito and he would doze off occasionally during the hour-long appointment. Once, when I realised he was nodding off, I just stopped talking and he fell deeper and deeper into sleep! Normally, when this happened I'd just speak a few words a little louder which would bring him round, but this time I let him sleep until he woke himself up snoring. I didn't have the nerve back then to say anything. I don't know what's funnier, his embarrassment or me developing a complex about being boring, which is how he got away with it – I wasn't going to tell anyone!

Cara had an appointment to see her psychiatrist and to get there she had to drive about eight miles, but this day she was very depressed and consumed with nervousness, anxiety and confusion. She knew that she wasn't well enough to drive, but there seemed to be no other option. Cara 'phoned the psychiatrist's receptionist and explained that she was very depressed, very unwell and wasn't able to drive. The receptionist replied "Start walking!"

If you're very unwell it's hard to get yourself out of the house to a doctor's appointment, but these

## Bi-Polar on Benefits

visits offer hope, hope that you've existed on since the last pointless appointment. It's worse if you have to drive and worse still, if you have to use public transport (way too stressful). But you force yourself to go, you classify it as a 'must do' on your 'to do' list.

What is it the experts say about avoiding stress? Oh yes.

*"Although Bi-polar disorder is not caused by stress, stressful situations can trigger episodes of mania or depression in those with the condition."*

*"Prevention. Some useful tips included. Avoid stressful situations which may trigger an episode of mania or depression."*

*Taken from the NHS Direct Website's Health Encyclopaedia, under Bipolar Disorder.*


## A Stunner and I'm Not Talking Gorgeous!

On this particular appointment with my psychiatrist, Dr P, there were two others who sat in, J, Senior (Community) Mental Health Practitioner and a new psychiatrist from overseas, learning the English ropes, if I didn't mind.

I was suicidal and I needed help – I was scaring myself. I don't find it easy to ask for help. I usually shut myself away and cope, but this time I had no desire to live and no voices of reason left to hear and that's a dangerous mindset. I sought help for no other reason than I have a son who needs me.

Dr P asked me what medication I was taking in a 'remind me' kind of way, then asked what dosage I was taking, whether I was married, had a job. It was as if she'd never seen me before. I could barely speak and all the answers she needed were in her notes in front of her. I could barely make eye contact. I'd had enough, I'd given it my best shot, I'd been dealt a tough hand this time round and I didn't want to go on any further, I couldn't, I didn't know how. Throwing the towel in; run out of gauntlets, sorry. I became agitated and angry at her incompetence (which is how it appeared at the time) and I answered back. I was frustrated and tearful – I knew she wasn't going to do anything to help me and I had waited weeks to see her.

She rambled on for yonks about being a good mother, eating properly and other related crap that made no sense to my brain. No reference at all was made to my suicidal feelings. She didn't seem to be treating this as an emergency appointment with a severely depressed, suicidal patient.

Much to my surprise she started to close the meeting until J very politely suggested that I explain my suicidal intentions, which I did reluctantly. Dr P reacted as though she'd heard my television viewing intentions for the evening and asked me whether I'd like to increase my dose. My body felt heavier, another slate filter slid over my view, my brain shut down another programme. I looked

## Bi-Polar on Benefits

zombie-like. She told me to go home, prepare a nice dinner for my son and this would make me feel much better and come back in six weeks. J interjected again suggesting that owing to the severity of the depression that was gripping me, the suicidal intentions and the suicide plan, I should perhaps be seen sooner rather that later (or too late). Dr P seemed puzzled, but agreed. I was given an appointment for two weeks hence (better than six). Thank God J was there, normally you see them alone at a time when you are weak, vulnerable and easily dismissed. J can't do much about these situations, her hands are tied. She does, after all, work for the psychiatrist in effect. But she tried and that in itself was a great comfort. I walked home alone, crossing roads without looking because if a car hit me it would be a blessing and it wouldn't be my fault! Looking back, if I'd had the wherewithal to have made a complaint about Dr P I would have done, but if I'd had the wherewithal to do that I wouldn't have needed her in the first place.

I got over that depressive period; I didn't kill myself, obviously! I'm off the Suicide List and back onto the Functioning List where I am right now, very depressed but functioning. Functioning means you can get something, anything with a calorific value down your neck be it chocolate, alcohol, biscuits or Caesar Salads, no matter.

I have many experiences to relate but fortunately for you I can't remember them owing to a few random psychological fugues along the way (when your brain deletes whole experiences and everything to do with them that are too painful to bear). It's a self-preservation, damage-limitation thing. Some of the good bits go as well.

**Do I Know You?**

For example, whilst in a psychiatric clinic I became friends with Sue, as did Cara. We had many laughs apparently, sitting in the coffee lounge, smoking (there's never anything else to do). When I met her again, shortly after we'd been discharged, I didn't remember her and was astounded to hear that we'd spent so much time together. I didn't even recognise her face. I got to know her all over again and realised why I'd liked her the first time round!

A few years ago I went to Lanzarote apparently. I have no memory of it and I was even more surprised to find out I'd been to Bulgaria, skiing!

After my NHS experience, J discovered I had private health insurance, so I was packed off to a private mental health clinic in the countryside. It had once been a country hotel with tennis courts, swimming pool and en-suite rooms. It was all a bit run down and tired and its atmosphere seemed weighted – probably all the sadness it had absorbed over the years. My sister later told me that it was the most depressing, run-down, neglected place she'd ever seen, but I thought it was lovely. And they didn't mind that I more or less

## Bi-Polar on Benefits

moved into their greenhouse with most of their indoor plants which I systematically re-potted and killed (I later found out), but it kept me happy. The psychiatrist there, Dr D, monitored my medication, I saw him once a week.

The clinic had it's own posse of therapists. I was sat in front of V twice a week for two years, initially as an in-patient and then as an out-patient. In all honesty I have no idea whatsoever what that woman said or did for me. I remember she was incredibly cold and sterile – it was purely business. Nobody monitored or evaluated my progress or her methods except for J. Though she was probably risking her position, J spoke to V on the 'phone and gave her a good pasting apparently. I don't know what she said to her but I know it would have been good, J's a clever woman and knows her stuff. After about eight weeks in Sutton Manor, J was told that there was no hope for me, they had to write me off, but J wasn't having any of it. Anyway, upshot was, I never went back, thank God and J found me a new psychiatrist. When you are severely depressed it is pointless to undergo psychological therapies. You would be too ill, too confused and too shut down to be reached. But there's money to be made in having your patients counselled and psychologically probed. I was even made to undergo marriage counselling at Sutton Manor with my estranged husband – J, again outraged, thought it was cruel and unethical and said as much.

Despite the clinic's shortcomings in the areas of mental health it did have one thing absolutely right, the location – it was secluded. If you're in a position to need hospital then you're really not coping and any kind of responsibility weakens you further. Even a simple responsibility like washing is not possible. Just seeing the iron or the vacuum turns you cold. A peaceful place where there are no reminders of life to paralyse you is the perfect setting for a badly depressed and terrified soul. Of course, I have no idea what medications they gave me in the drug line-ups every day, but who cares! Sutton Manor closed down not long after I was there.

## Barbarism, Toast & Rich Tea Biscuits

Dr S, my new private psychiatrist sent me to a clinic in London for electro convulsive therapy or ECT. It's a method of treatment used for severely depressed patients. It is still considered a last resort treatment by many specialists. Under general anaesthetic an electrical current is passed through the brain via two probes placed one on each temple. It is thought to jolt the brain into performing normally again, as I understand.

It was the worst experience of hospitalisation I've ever had or would want to have. On a ward on a floor there was me and one other. A young man with a beautiful smile. I felt sorry for him. He was lonely, I guessed, and confused like me. Apart from chance meetings in the kitchen over the rich

## Bi-Polar on Benefits

tea biscuits I avoided him. There were no staff on this floor and no one ever came except to get me for my ECT treatments. I wondered if they knew I was there. It was so cold.

The street-fronting restaurant, on the other hand, was bright, airy and full of happy people lunching and chatting. It was several minutes before I managed to convince myself that I hadn't accidentally stumbled into a real café, several minutes of dense, thundering fear and panic. Were these people London's fashionably depressed? These people didn't look depressed, because if they were, they wouldn't have been able to be there. No one spoke to me, no one helped me. It was an overwhelming experience, not least because I didn't know the ropes. I couldn't eat there again - toast and Rich Tea biscuits from then on - something you'll always find on a ward, private or NHS. No one seemed to notice at £400 a night, plus treatments.

## ECT (Electro Convulsive Therapy)

I believe that I was pretty zombied when it was decided that ECT was my best option. They'd tried all kinds of drugs from each of the three major drug families including Lithium and nothing seemed to be getting through to me. Apparently I was just an empty shell. Hollow eyes. I don't remember any of this, I have only tiny glimpses of what happened, but not enough to piece anything back together. I think the ECT did help a bit, it wasn't dramatic but it was a foot up. The hospital care was appalling. I told Dr S, who apologised and said he would never send anyone there again. Yeah right. Not long after the ECT treatment I lost my job and so my private medical cover. I couldn't book any more appointments to see him and I never heard from him again, not even a note to ask how I was doing, which still surprises me to this day. Did he not wonder if his diagnosis was right, if the treatment worked? I'm embarrassed at my naiveté in thinking a medical doctor might be interested enough in his chosen career to want to make someone better! But no, it's just business. First lesson learned - they don't care.

I'd love to tell you to be careful and choose your psychiatrist wisely, but if you're in a position to really need one, you'd be in no fit state to judge. And anyway, how would you choose? The one reporting the least suicides?

The private medical insurers don't evaluate the care you're getting with their money, it seems. Perhaps they're too busy trying to find a way to get you off their books. They spent, on me alone, in two years about £80k and the rest, and for what?

**NHS vs. Private**

I believe in a national health service and I mostly dislike private healthcare, particularly in the mental health sector. I loathe that money is the decider when it comes to ill-health or wellness, life or death, death next week or death in 10 years.

For the record, I have not been overly impressed with the relatively short period of private treatment I received and I am now grateful to be under the umbrella of a national health system, if only I could get it to work for me.

Even with a private psychiatrist, in an emergency you may be taken to an NHS Accident & Emergency department where you might be admitted to a ward and you'd be under the care of the NHS; a new psychiatrist of course and, very likely, new medication. I like the potential consistency of an NHS and you know they're not doing it for the money whereas it seems quite the contrary in the private sector.

## A Fresh Start

I moved from Hertfordshire to West Sussex (don't ask) and was told that the Herts team would liaise with my new doctors in West Sussex, there would be a proper hand-over. All I had to do to get the ball rolling was to register with the new GP. I felt re-assured.

It was a good few months before I did register. I was reluctant to open up this can of worms yet again and considered not seeking medical treatment at all, I didn't think I had the strength, but it turns out I did. My GP duly referred me to a psychiatrist at the local hospital. Here we go again.

I waited for an appointment and as the weeks passed I sunk into a deeper depression. My new home, my fresh start wasn't having the desired effect, it didn't make me feel hopeful and positive as I had thought. In reality I had moved prisons. It was a long wait for an appointment, during which time I became really depressed – I wanted to give up. I had stopped taking my anti-depressants for two reasons. One, I knew that the new psychiatrist would try me on something new and, having rid my body of the old anti-depressant, I'd be able to start them straight away and two, because Cara had been told by Professor Farmer at the Maudsley that anti-depressants can cause rapid-cycling in Bi-polars.

Eventually I got an appointment see a psychiatrist. It would be different this time, I told myself, I would be allocated a good psychiatrist, not one that doesn't hear you, not one that doesn't even look at you, but it all went tits up. How's ya luck?

Initial consultations are routine, he asks a few questions and you try to tell him what you think he needs to hear, what's relevant, what's pertinent, whilst he reads something. I asked him if it was possible to have community support (in the form of a community nurse, or social worker, as I'd had in Hertfordshire which had been very beneficial) and he told me that we would discuss this at the next appointment, he prescribed an anti-depressant. I

## Bi-Polar on Benefits

would be sent, by mail, an appointment for four weeks hence. I refused to feel disappointed, but I was.

The second appointment was a disaster. He would treat me for depression, Bi-polar wasn't an option. He told me that I was depressed owing to money worries, full stop. I asked him if there was any support available, counsellors, CBT practitioners, a community nurse. No, there was no support for me, but I could attend a day centre I where I would spend the day with others like me, the depressed, the manic and the social forgotten-abouts, but I'm either too ill to get there or too well to need it. What do you do?

As I sat in his office I cried quietly, I'm ashamed to say, any hope dashed. He wrote notes. I began to shout at him, sort of, about the futility of his post as my psychiatrist given that he would not, could not do anything to help me. He had no counsellors, therapists or psychologists to refer me to, no community support, no tools for his trade. That's like a painter without a brush or a dentist without a drill. What's the point of you sitting there, I said, I can get prescriptions from my GP? He shrugged. Again I cried quietly, hunched in the chair. He wrote notes. As I sat there, hopeless, I felt the urge to dive through the window, end it all. I held on to the arms of the chair. Then the urge to thrust my arm through the glass door of his bookcase. Really scary shit! I didn't tell him, there was no point. The only thing he said to me, three times, was 'would you like to wash your face?' No I fucking wouldn't.

## Sandy Knox

We sat in silence, he carried on writing. I was put in a room on my own, at my request, where I pulled myself together, as you do, and discreetly left 30 minutes later. The receptionist checked on me twice whilst I was in the room. No-one noticed when I left, or 'phoned to see if I had made it home safely. I drove home in a trance. I would receive notification of the next appointment by mail.

I didn't receive an appointment letter, instead I received a letter telling me that I had missed my third appointment, an appointment I didn't know anything about. I blamed myself. I must have forgotten. I telephoned to apologise and was told I'd be sent another appointment by mail. What a waste of a stamp, etc, but there you go.

I decided to pursue some community support myself during a brief period of stoic determination and after making a 'phone call or three I was given an appointment for a mental health social worker to make a home-visit. I was so relieved, at last some support, someone to help keep me keep going, give me hope. On the day of the visit I was nervous and nauseous. A male stranger would be coming into my home; I would have to regurgitate my medical history, etc. I might cry. I paced the floor, wrung my hands, sat at the table, got up from the table, paced some more, smoked cigarettes. Eventually I sat down, where I could see the front door. It was a gloomy day inside and out. A couple of hours later I finally accepted that he wasn't

## Bi-Polar on Benefits

coming. I went to bed. He never came. I never learned why.

*"The exact cause of Bi-polar disorder is unknown. However, it is thought that a complex mix of physical, environmental and social factors are involved."*

*Taken from the NHS Direct Website's Health Encyclopaedia, under Bipolar Disorder.*

Two months after my last appointment with Dr M I received a letter telling me that, yet again, I'd missed my appointment. I was livid. Finally, I was given an appointment with Dr M and a social worker – the point of the meeting was to discuss the failed appointments. Dr M apologised profusely for the mix-up with the appointment system; I must have fallen through the net. Shit happens! The social worker tried to give me a lecture about positive thinking, but I cut her dead, asking her not to patronise me, I was in no mood for that text book clap-trap, but I was reassured that the appointment mix up would never happen again. Result. Appointments are important. They are a lifeline, milestones, things to aim for. But it happened again, another letter arrived regarding a missed appointment. Annoyed, I wrote back telling him that I was considering taking legal action on the grounds of medical neglect. I bet that went down well!

The next two appointments were cancelled by me, because I was simply too ill to get there, unable to leave my house, unable to drive, only just able to use the phone to cancel (failing that I would have sent a fax). I was given another appointment for four months hence – this meant that I would remain unseen for eight months! I must have really pissed him off about the law suit thing! It stunned me. It crushed me. I was sinking further. And on top of that I discovered that my Benefits had been stopped three months earlier, yet again. I was numb, panicky, even cried on the 'phone to Cara. Cara was worried, she tells me now and, on my behalf, 'phoned the clinic's Receptionist (very brave) to ask her, plead with her, to secure me a second opinion. It worked. I saw Dr P, a Consultant Psychiatrist.

My boyfriend, Tel, accompanied me who, as it turned out, was very useful as he could relate and confirm symptoms that I wasn't necessarily aware of. Dr P was different. He didn't sit at his desk reading and writing, ignoring me as I spoke, he wheeled his chair away from his desk and conversed with me like I was a human being, no really! He listened to me, to my boyfriend and diagnosed, without hesitation, Bi-polar disorder and at that time severe. The relief was palpable. It had only taken four years to get an NHS diagnosis! Unfortunately for me, he was a locum consultant psychiatrist and I wouldn't be seeing him again, but I had a diagnosis that nobody could deny.

# Bi-Polar on Benefits

## Nobody Likes a Label

Well I do. I may be labelled a manic-depressive, but the label means a lot to me. I presented my label to my inner judge and jury, and they, without hesitation excused me, at last, for my past sins and wicked pleasures. It has set me free from the baggage that has hindered me for so long. With hindsight I can see why I failed at so many of the things I tried. Why chasing my dreams came to nothing and why life was such a struggle. It wasn't my fault. I know this now. I'll wear the t-shirt, if you like!


## Sickening

What sickens me is that there's an NHS mental health unit at the Maudsley Hospital in London, headed by Professor Farmer. I know she can get me better because she told Cara she could get her better and Cara's more severe than me!

Cara's Consultant referred her to see Professor Farmer. The Professor arranged for the next available bed. Cara would be admitted in the summer for an eight week stay. During that eight weeks she would be de-toxed and re-medicated, counselled and CBT'd. Wow! For the first time in a long time I sensed relief in Cara's voice. She felt that at last an end to this crazy life could be a positive one. The power of hope!

Three times her consultant requested funding for her treatment from the relevant department and three times has been turned down. 'Lack of funds' - only 'extreme' cases admitted. All her hopes dashed. After each refusal Cara became really depressed. You would, wouldn't you?

Cara can be very manic one day, then very depressed for a week, then a bit manic for two days, then mixed and manic within a day, then flat for a morning and very manic by the afternoon, really manic by evening and depressed as hell the next day.

This ultra rapid cycling can go on for weeks at a time, I've witnessed it. If that's not extreme, what is?

# Bi-Polar on Benefits

## Chapter 4: Social Care Experience

If you can keep your head when all about you are losing theirs, then you're doing a damn sight better than me.

## Cut to the Chase

You find yourself paralysed with depression and your circumstances require you to seek help in the form of State Benefits in order to keep a roof over your head. You have to telephone the Jobcentreplus whereupon you will be cut off. You try again and are passed to someone who will help you complete the necessary forms over the 'phone, then you'll be cut off. You try again, but you can't speak to the same person, you have to speak to someone new and start again. You don't think you can try again today. You don't think you'll be able to speak coherently, you might cry. How humiliating is that? You sit there numb, exhausted, you can barely keep your eyes open. You need a bed. You have to lie down. You tell yourself that you failed, yet again, you failed. The telephone becomes an object of suspicion and invokes panic; it is avoided. It may be some days before you can face the 'phone again. The forms contain questions that are personal and sometimes your answers will stir emotion. They are forms I've completed many times before, they have more copies of my information than I can remember.

## Sandy Knox

I can picture myself sitting at the table on a grey, wet day, head down, tears falling, trying to keep my voice steady for a stranger on the other end of a 'phone who wants to know details of my 'illness', my circumstances, my doctors, my son. After the 'phone call you are sent, by mail, a copy of the completed form for you to amend, add to, check and sign, which you then return with an array of identification; utility bills, passport, drivers license, pay slip (and only originals will be accepted, no photo-copies). So, if you also need help paying for housing, school meals or council tax, for example, you will have to contact other departments and complete more forms that require original identification papers. This process, with only one set of originals, has to be completed before the automatic deadline closes your case. Contacting the Jobcentreplus to apply for Benefits would test the mettle of anyone.

It shames me to have to admit to being dependent on State Benefits, but there it is. Benefits keep me going and I am grateful to live in a country that provides this support, but sadly there have been gross inconsistencies that have had devastating consequences. Four times now my Benefits have been stopped without notice. Months later, a computer-generated letter in a brown envelope tells me my circumstances have changed thus Benefits stopped.

After the first time I discovered my Benefits had been stopped, I studied my bank statements and with my heart in my mouth realised that the

## Bi-Polar on Benefits

payments had stopped nearly ten months earlier – I had been too unwell to deal with my finances in all that time, but as all my commitments are automated by direct debit I presumed everything was going smoothly. My heart sank, my stomach knotted, my mind raced with the complications and consequences. Why hadn't they warned me? And how have my circumstances changed? I was stunned, shell-shocked. Where would I get money from? I sunk into a deeper depression, panic and fear consuming me. I wrote myself a credit card cheque.

What is it that the medical experts say about avoiding stress, oh yes!

*"Bi-polar disorder may also be triggered by overwhelming problems in everyday life, such as problems to do with money, work and relationships."*

*Taken from the NHS Direct Website's Health Encyclopaedia, under Bipolar Disorder.*

It was days before I was well enough to 'phone them. When I did I was met with the usual unanswered 'phone, followed by department passing, followed by being cut off. When I eventually got through I was passed to a Sheffield call-centre. The man who dealt with me was very kind as I explained my situation; I was close to tears; poor guy. He advised me to apply for Incapacity Benefit so I completed the form over the 'phone whereupon I had to disclose the usual personal, sensitive information. I was close to breaking point. I was panicking inside, desperate and wanting to cry. I wanted to tell him that I didn't think I could do this any more, that I wanted to give up, at the end. To just forget the whole thing and I'll go quietly to my bed and pray to God to stop my heart. But I didn't. I was given a 'phone number for a crisis loan, which, as I remember, was about £10 to be collected daily. I wrote myself another credit card cheque.

Two weeks later I received a letter informing me that I wasn't entitled to Incapacity Benefit and suggested I claim for Income Support, if I liked. I numbed over. I would have to wait for the form to arrive in the mail, complete it and send it back (even though the form I completed for Incapacity Benefit two weeks prior contained the necessary information). Do they not communicate? Meanwhile, the housing benefit and council tax benefit was stopped, it's a knock-on effect. I wrote myself another credit card cheque.

The imminent paperwork and fruitless 'phone calls with officious, unemotional voices loomed like a monster and had to be confronted. I was terrified. I feared losing my house. I feared the search for a new home. I feared red letters, court injunctions, bankruptcy and whatever else happens to you when you go down the pan. I feared hospitalisation. I feared the aloneness and I loathed myself and manic depression. It took weeks to get my Benefits re-instated, though I'm still in the dark as to why they were abruptly

## Bi-Polar on Benefits

stopped and I'm still paying interest on the credit card cheques which, at this rate, I'll still be paying off long after I'm dead!

One of the effects of depression is that you can't face anything and so you can't keep on top of everyday things. Mail piles up because you're not able or brave enough to touch it, never mind deal with it. You feel unsafe because everything around you is scary. Sometimes I go without cigarettes because the fear of what's involved in actually buying them is far greater than going without – my brain simply ignores the addiction, shuts down that programme, because it has enough to deal with.

I can't always use a 'phone, answer the door, take a shower, eat. It's not always like that, but often enough to really screw up my life.

## Chapter 5: Quality of Life

I think I'm three people, not in the multiple personality sense, but as a way of differentiating between me, manic-me and depressed-me. It's key to the whole 'living with manic depression' thing; I need to differentiate between the three in order to identify potential triggers so as to avoid them. Normal me, is central with manic and depressed either side. I sit in the middle, like an umpire in a pointless, never-ending game of self-destruction, watching all the to-ing and fro-ing and trying to keep my eye on the ball. I try to communicate with them, reason with them, compromise. Sometimes it works, but most of the time it doesn't.

## Reclusion, Isolation, Solitude

I didn't sit down one day and decide to isolate myself, I seem to have slipped into this way of coping with, and understanding my moods and the opposing 'personalities' that are mania and depression.

*I have a party to go to. I was invited eight days ago when I was feeling happy and well and I cordially accepted. This leads to a flurry of catalogue-browsing for the perfect outfit, as you do – all very exciting. The party is now 6 hours away and I'm depressed, anxious and scared, been like this for about three days and it feels like it's getting worse,*

## Bi-Polar on Benefits

*everything going greyer. I don't understand why it has happened, I was looking forward to the party. Looking forward to dressing up and seeing old friends, having a laugh. I'd almost decided what to wear bar a few accessories. I bought the gift. What happened? I'm terrified and I don't want anyone, anyone to see me this way. Yet I have no choice, I tell myself, I have to go, they're counting on me. I promised. I tried to tempt myself with the promise of feeling a bit better once I'd showered, but the thought of standing naked, vulnerable in the shower, my body violated and diluted made me feel worse, even panicky.*

I didn't go to the party, but I did manage, after three hours, to get myself to 'phone. Vomited afterwards, but I did it.

Depressions have scuppered many, many plans. At fifteen I studied for my exams under a dense, numbing fog of depression. I was new to it, inexperienced and so I became it, it controlled me and, as it happened, steered me into a nose-dive which lasted four years. I stayed on at school to do A-levels after my dismal O-level results, but I only attended classes for a few days and formally left the following week. I enrolled, immediately, into a college for a variety of two-year courses, for no reason other than my parents, who were on holiday at the time, were due back and I did not want to face my Dad with the news that I had left school. I dutifully attended college, but soon sank into a persistent depression and would miss the odd class, the odd day and sometimes the odd week. I was doing my best; home-life was largely unpleasant, owing in part to a father who was bad-tempered, a brother who either ignored me or was mean to me, a jerk of a boyfriend whom I couldn't, for one reason or another, get rid of and a mother who idolised my sister and craved my brother's attention whilst I got the brunt of her 'complete cow, topped with women's lib' phase. I left just a few months before the exams. The relief of finally making the decision to quit college removed an enormous pressure and lightened considerably the burden of guilt.

But I recovered, slowly, and by the following summer, buzzing with hope, I enrolled again on a different variety of two-year A-level courses. I didn't last a year. I didn't want to give up on my dreams and plans, I hasten to add, I didn't give up on them, I gave in to depression. I had missed too many classes and I just couldn't do it any more. I chose not to take the exams because I knew I'd fail miserably and I'd rather not have an exam certificate at all than have a failed one. But that's just me.

I spent the next year unemployed, on the dole and in love with the man who stole my heart from my jerk of a boyfriend. He had a motorbike and a whole crowd of lovely motorbike friends. Camping, bike shows and drunken nights – I blossomed. I was loved and safe and having fun, life started to feel worth while and with that my self-confidence and hope grew.

## Bi-Polar on Benefits

Out of the blue, I suggested to my boyfriend that we move to South Africa, but had second thoughts and decided on America instead. And that's what we did. I embarked on another college course, a one-year, intensive secretarial course, for no other reason than I thought a secretary could get a job almost anywhere in the world, and I could qualify in a year. I felt hopeful and a new life in America dangling in front of me would ensure I finished the course with something to show for it. I didn't attend every day; in fact I missed many days and sometimes weeks for the usual reason. The depressions always got me and for no apparent reason, there were no apparent triggers. Life was good, wasn't it? I had a lovely boyfriend and a future in America, I was excited. I passed all the exams and did quite well despite my poor attendance. But I'm not proud, necessarily, it was a very easy course.

I lived in New York for four years before returning to the UK. Life there was much the same as it was here – I was unable to leave my problems in England. Deep depressions would ambush me, hold me down and drain everything that was good and eventually I'd be spat out, shell-shocked. I'm pleased I experienced my short emigration, it was good for me all in all.

When I decided I wanted to have a child, I didn't give much thought, if any, to the possibility of my becoming post-nataly depressed. Should I have done? After all, I didn't know I had Bi-polar back then, but I knew I was prone to regular, crippling depressions. Anyway, I didn't question it.

There are three chapters to the whole having a baby thing, there's the pregnancy, the birth and all the years after the birth. I loved being pregnant despite two to three months of unbearable sickness. I loved the fact that a life was being created. Fascinated by the fact that a new human being was growing inside me.

The birth was an exhaustive, painful, thirty-three hour ordeal but it was really good fun! I can't remember when I last had such a good laugh. Sometimes I laughed so much I was hysterical. Eventually, after every contraction I'd burst out laughing. I laughed and poked fun at any and all of the many doctors and nurses. They all ignored me, which I also thought was funny. I giggled quietly all the way to the theatre, but when my husband presented himself to me wearing a green gown with hat and mask I burst into fits of hysterical laughter so much so that the nurse had to ask me to stop laughing because I was rocking the table and the surgeon was ready to go in, so to speak. My response to the nurse who said, "you have a beautiful boy" was "do you know, I'd forgotten what I'd come in for!" which I thought was hilarious. Then I wanted everyone in the theatre to know I was truly amazed that the operation was over so suddenly because I hadn't even realised it had started.

## Bi-Polar on Benefits

I can only put my behaviour down to the pain relieving gas and air combination (aka Laughing Gas) on tap, all you can eat! It affects each individual differently, but I believe I was manic, triggered by the stress of a very difficult labour and so the gas and air complemented my mania beautifully. Fantastic stuff! Where can I buy it?

When I saw my son for the very first time the hysterics and silliness vaporised and I fell in love and have remained so ever since. I never suffered with Post-Natal Depression, in fact I was largely depression-free for about a year. Mothering came naturally to me and I enjoyed every minute (well, except for school plays, coffee mornings, uniforms, raffle tickets, child care, swimming lessons and other mothers). Perhaps I am lucky.

I live with my son. I rarely leave the house. My 'phone doesn't ring and only the postman comes to my door (with nasty brown envelopes). I have a poor, usually non-existent sense of smell and taste and an erratic appetite, so eating isn't always a priority. I have no social life. I make no plans. My future is here, I'm living it. I see no change. I have no job and no prospects of work. I have no money, in fact worse, I have debt. I don't have anything to look forward to, that's just how it is.

I think my anger and frustration are evident to others. I think I wear them like a coat. I am angry and I am frustrated and I can't hide it like I can my feelings of depression and mania - old hand at that. Anger and frustration frighten me so I have overcome this hurdle by removing everyone but shopkeepers from my life. Which, as it turns out, has helped with many other troublesome aspects of my mind like zero self-confidence, esteem and belief, I have removed the risk.

*I'm lying in bed this day. It's 1.40pm. I have already been up and fed the dogs, but it has taken all my energy. I'm depressed and emotionless and lonely. I becomes we and we talk together.*

*Come on, why don't you have a shower?*
*Can't be bothered.*
*You always feel better after a shower.*
*What's the point?*
*Okay then, let's do something in the garden?*
*I'm not going outside today.*
*Come on, we've got to do something to get out of this. Have a shower, do your hair, put some make-up on and walk the dogs. You'll feel great if your hair's done.*
*I don't want to. I can't.*
*Why?*
*I don't know I just can't. I don't have the energy or desire to drag myself anywhere. I just want to go to bed.*
*Okay then, we'll try to sleep and then have a shower and walk the dogs.*
*Maybe.*

# Bi-Polar on Benefits

## Holiday Hell

I've been on many holidays in my time, to many different places. I haven't been lucky, I've worked hard. Sad though it is, I've actually only properly enjoyed a few that weren't blighted at some point by a depression or mania. Sometimes an emotionless, sad, dark depression or one with overwhelming fear and a sense of impending doom so intense you can feel it pushing you down. Or a mania that has you buying case-loads of crap or plain making an arse of yourself. Of course, I've always had to try to hide it, not least because I didn't always understand it.

I remember a holiday some years back which I had been looking forward to with great excitement. I would 'phone my friend, with whom I was going, almost every day and we'd talk about the holiday, the travel, what we'd wear, as you do: I was manic. I couldn't have been looking forward to it more, but when we got to our first destination, I was consumed by fear, which triggered panic, which made me anxious. I felt unsafe, though I feared nothing. I felt threatened though nothing was threatening me. I felt exhausted and devastated with disappointment.

Being out of my comfort zone was possibly a trigger, regardless, the reality was that I was in a bad way and my comfort zone, my home was 10 days and a plane ride away. Could I survive 10 days? How? How was I going to do this? After a couple of days, walking the shops, smiling, wearing happy clothes, drinks round the bar, I could hide it no more. I couldn't keep up the 'I'm normal' façade and, as per usual, I would sink deep into a fairly visible depression and excuse myself from the holiday-making, which doesn't go down well. I hid in my strange bed in my strange room in a strange country with just the flicker of a hopeful thought that my mood might lift before we leave and then lay in fear of that very thing, wracked with and wrecked by self-loathing.

Hadn't I been looking forward to the holiday? Hadn't I been excited? Hadn't I planned my wardrobe and my make-up? What the hell happened? I have lovely memories of the few holidays that were relatively 'normal'!

**My Normal**

Normal, for me, is simply not being depressed or manic. Within the realms of normalcy are ups and downs; not nice but not life threatening, not extreme. I'm realistic about normal. When, if my mood stabilises and I'm back to my normal self, life will not necessarily be easier. When I'm better I'll be confronted by another huge mountain; the struggle to rebuild my life and secure a future. I can't even bring myself to think about it.

How can a doctor get me better if he doesn't know what my better looks like? How could he, he didn't know me when I was well and I don't recall ever

## Bi-Polar on Benefits

being asked about it? What does his better look like? I've lived with depression and mania all my life so how do I know what my better looks like? I know who I am at the core, the essence of me and the me who is better is confident and calm and in control. I'm studious, quiet, a deep thinker. I like challenges. I like to set myself projects with deadlines. Deadlines turn me on, so to speak. I like order. I like organising. I like my own company. I don't need anyone. I exercise my creative mind regularly. I love being naughty, I love fun and laughter. I love music and lyrics. I love writing. I love contemplating, philosophising and pontificating (much to the dismay of my boyfriend who thinks I talk bollocks – what does he know?). Anyway, this is what better looks like for me so I suppose it's only fair I tell the doctor so we can finally sing in harmony from the same song sheet!

I've had a normal-ish few weeks. Stable, calm and content to potter along. I even told the doctor I felt quite good. I wore make-up, proper make-up. I went to the shops. I started and finished a decorating project! I took care of some paperwork and sorted some urgent financial matters, not all, but some. I steam cleaned my carpet and the bathroom walls. I'm hopelessly in love with Tel after two and half years! I've turned the radio on! I appear well. The doctor will be pleased.

But actually I am not well. Not well at all. I can't use the 'phone and I can't speak to anyone. I can't for reasons unbeknown to me. I have not spoken to Cara in the last four, five, six weeks and I worry about that. I haven't spoken to my parents, I feel guilty about that. I have created a micro-life for myself, a little bell jar under which I can do all kinds of things, but I can't speak to anyone and I only go out if I really have to and preferably with Tel. There is no 'phone in my bell jar, just a couple of hot-lines! Occasionally I have been able to venture outside into the garden, but outside is too scary to think about, full stop. I appear well to my boyfriend and son. But something rumbles constantly within, something that may be about to loom and the air in here is stale. I have spells of uncertainty, fear, panic and doubt that cause shakiness. I can hide it. I forgot to tell that to the doctor.

On the odd days that I have felt normal I have been pretty down, not depressed, per se. Why, because my life's shit? Because in normal-state I can plainly, calmly and logically see the state of my life, my dilemma, my dire circumstances, which would depress anyone, and, what's worse, there seems to be sod-all I can do about it. I just have to battle for consistent medical treatment and support, because logically, my becoming well is the first step.

In normal-state I have to live in a world that was created for my manic-depressed state, a life of coping mechanisms, of lonely silence. I find myself not knowing what I should do, only what I shouldn't do. I have to tread carefully because I live in fear of a shift into depression or mania so I monitor and observe myself through the day skirting the dangerous triggers. That rules out contacting friends and family, going for a coffee and a browse

## Bi-Polar on Benefits

round the shops or playing with one of my dust-gathering hobbies and interests. So I walk the dogs on my own, or watch day-time telly on my own, do some cleaning and washing, try to catch up. It's boring and lonely and my brain cries out for stimulation. I have de-sensitised myself from life outside whilst I'm within the four walls of my home. I'm cut off, secluded and I feel safe. Everything's fine inside my home. Any contact with the world beyond my door and I can't cope. I have lost confidence and my ability to socialise, even my desire to socialise, but the illness itself isn't the cause, it's an effect, a wound from a battle, if you like. My confidence is low from years of holing myself away, hiding from prying eyes in case I humiliate myself in public or say or do something I shouldn't. There has to be more to life than this.


**Make-Believe**

*The atmosphere is smokey from cigarettes. It's dark with bright twinkly lights like diamonds in red, yellow and white. I'm sitting in the corner, near the door, lounged with one hand on the table, just sitting in the sexy smoke listening to the music which is heaving with beat. There are hungry men everywhere and I look hot, really hot. I'm a focal point and almost everyone who passes takes a look at me. They ponder who I might be because they think I must be somebody.*

That's my definition of a fantasy, a little play I perform in my head that I sit back and enjoy. That particular one was played out in a car, hence I had to be sitting down with one hand up and my music is always blaring anyway, but of course, I don't smoke in the car anymore, 'cos I'm told it's not allowed!

I don't know how much time I spend inside these fantastical thoughts. They don't last long, shortly after that I pretended I was one of the Top Gear team testing a new car. This is how it went, I had won a competition for a drive in a reasonably priced car and as I was so good, and thinking they needed a female representative Test Driver, Mr Clarkson had chosen me! You know the rest!

I have fantasised about what it will be like when I'm famous! Don't know why I'll be famous or what I will have done, good or bad! I think about the photo-shoots, the beauty treatments. The people I'll meet. As fantasies go, and mine are always fairytale, it sounds harmless enough but they can actually turn out to have devastating effects because I'm wasting precious time in them. This depresses me and I berate myself for allowing these ridiculous, seemingly unstoppable daydreams. And as for fame, I can't think of anything worse. So I waste time fantasising about negative things instead. Of course, fantasising is just that, a fantasy. Fame or notoriety is the last thing I want. In my fantasy I am well, happy, confident and independent, young and slim with lots of nice shoes and bags. That's not reality, unfortunately, that's just make-believe.

# Bi-Polar on Benefits

## Social Interaction

I do long for social interaction. I sometimes crave the company of friends, but the risk of anxiety and perhaps a zoom into mania are too high, I haven't got the energy and the thought of the unfailing depression as a finale seals the deal. And anyway, I haven't got anything to talk about.

It's sad for me to have had to let go of all but a few people in my life. That, owing to my situation, it's the only way I can keep what's left of me together. The future scares me. It will be hard to rekindle some of those relationships because they won't be the same.

*I am depressed this day, been like it for months. I'm holed away, incommunicado. I can leave the house only to go to three specific places; the local shop, the vet and the school, if I have to. Although I'm depressed I feel strangely calm. Just an undercurrent of anxiety humming away. I am able to control the fear today – I've been able to put it on standby, it seems. There have been no nasty brown envelopes of late (not for a week anyway). I'm not worrying about my neglected bank account (out of sight, out of mind). I'm not feeling paranoid. My neighbours don't think I'm mysterious or famous! It takes a while to get my head around feeling a bit better.*

*I enjoy a cup of tea and a cigarette and a flick through the local free paper. I cleansed my face thoroughly, for a change, even considered a face pack. All is well. I wanted to do something enjoyable, something creative. I want to paint with my airbrush. It would be therapeutic and God knows I could do with the respite. But already I can feel the cogs of common sense creaking into action to put a dampener on everything. Common sense reminds me that my ironing basket is now an ironing cupboard; that I've been in West Sussex a year now and haven't finished unpacking; that I don't know where the hell I am with my finances.*

*It becomes a never ending bickering session in my head between two characters, one who insists I be responsible and the other who just wants to have a bit of fun, if only briefly.*

Despite ignoring the sensible nagging I didn't get to play with my airbrush. I couldn't concentrate. I spent the day confused, trying to prioritise what needed to be done. Is ironing so important? To relax would be so therapeutic.

*I pace the floor. I should eat something. I should check my bank account. I should 'phone the Jobcentreplus to find out why they've stopped my Benefits, again.*

I didn't even manage to prioritise a list that day and so achieved nothing. I hated myself. I couldn't look me in the mirror.

*I'm a waste of everybody's time. The lowest of the low. Useless. A failure. A parasite, of no use to man or beast.*

# Bi-Polar on Benefits

The next day my mood was similarly calm. The two characters compromised, so I did a bit of both; I opened my mail and I did some writing and was beside myself with joy, if only briefly, at the magnitude of my achievement.

## Shameful

Occasionally, out of sheer desperation and to pacify a frustrated mind, I play a game on my computer in which I can lose myself completely for a few hours. In this game I can build and control a flourishing Roman city, communicate with it's people and keep everyone happy, even the gods! It's an escape. But it doesn't look good, does it? A grown woman, sat at home on a Tuesday afternoon playing a computer game when there's a basket full of laundry, the sink's full of dishes and dinner not even considered. What can I say?

I know some of you have got it sussed. Like the text book says "surround yourself with people who understand you. Know what makes you happy. Find something you love to do. Eat properly, exercise and avoid stress, join a club and make new friends". Is that all? It sounds so simple. I admit that it is a situation for which I strive as I learn more about coping with Bi-polar, or just depression as it seems to be these days, but it's hard to make major life changes when you're depressed. It's hard to the point of impossible, because you either don't have the confidence and courage or you couldn't give a shit!

> It's got me in a stranglehold
> But hey, it's up to me, or so I'm told
> Is that the case, why didn't you say?
> I'll just pull myself together then
> And get on with my fucking day!

When I'm depressed I don't want to be in the company of anyone. I want to hide away and I don't want help, or at least it will come across that I don't want help. In truth, I do want help, but not from you or you or you. I don't know who can help me. My inability to seek help when I am unwell is worrying. If the depression deepens I hide further, there is no courage to reach out, reaching out is scary and humiliating and embarrassing and in my experience, pointless. But a deepening depression is a dangerous state to be in when you're alone and all you can hear in your head is the debate "do reasons to live outweigh reasons to die?".

*I'm normal this morning and I'm up early. God, it's such a relief. My mind is clear and quiet. I realise I had become accustomed to the deafening mutiny in my head. I gather some laundry and a cup that has been in my room for two weeks and head downstairs to make my first cup of tea of the day. While the kettle boils I empty the dishwasher and fill it up again. While the tea brews I put some washing in. Drinking tea at the table, I smoke a cigarette and flick, casually through a junk catalogue. I turn the radio on to catch the last*

## Bi-Polar on Benefits

*twenty minutes of Terry Wogan and I chuckle occasionally because he says such silly things. More tea finished, I decide to change the beds and clean the bathroom properly before mid-day. I eat lunch in front of the telly watching my muse, Judge Judy, for a slice of justice and some people to look down on for a change! I decide to walk the dogs thinking I'd get it over with, as you do; so I walk the dogs and quite enjoy the whole fresh air thing. I will feel invigorated. On my return and thinking it's the mature, responsible thing to do, I apply myself to my overflowing in-tray which I struggle across the room with. I sort it into two piles, filing and action, make a few 'phone calls, tick a few boxes and write a cheque. Job done. I feel good, as you would. I am thinking decisively and rationally and I can see things for what they are. I can see reality plain and clear. I sit at my table, in my chair, with my tea and my cigarette, a little make up, my hair, though brushed, is still in the shape it was when it left the pillow and I look around at the half-finished projects. The hatch, the floor, the second coat of paint, the garden, the list is long. I hear the silence. I'm so normal in my thinking, so level-headed that I can't help but look at the huge mountain ahead, it's staring at me. How will I ever get my life back on track? Where do I start? Dare I start? Regardless, I look up my bank account on the Internet.*

*Realistically, I have about six weeks left before I sink into a terminal overdraft, this is a shock. I think about getting back to work, but the implications and risks of a destabilised Bi-polar disorder leave me confused. It seems impossible to get back to work,*

*I feel stuck. The obstacles ahead are terrifying, constructing a CV with a seven year gap and out-of-date IT. Applying for a position, preparing for the interview, the interview itself, even the drive to the interview. My temperamental memory and recall. Sitting at the table, head in hands I feel physical fear. I can't face it, I know I can't. I'm not ready.*

I exercised "showing myself a little kindness" and told myself that it really was too early to be thinking about work and I felt much better, relieved, calmer.

After a proactive, hopeful day I saw what really lies ahead, nothing, so I had an early night.

**Bi-Polar Fashion**

I could definitely split my wardrobe into two. There's the manic collection and the depressed collection. The manic collection is colourful and sexy and has accessories. The depressed collection is dark, plain and body covering. When depressed the manic collection bothers me and I would not, could not imagine wearing any of it. When manic I wear what I like. Being caught out in manic clothes when a depression hits is one of those sickening experiences that leaves me panicking for safety, for home.

Cara is the perfect example of extreme, severe Bi-polar illness, sadly - not the greatest accolade but she is keen to be used as a model if it would help another sufferer because she's like that. Bi-polar

## Bi-Polar on Benefits

began for her with the onset of post-natal depression though like me, she suspects she has been so for most of her life. Prior to that she had been happy, materially successful, you know, big home, swimming pool, money, career, travel. Today she tells me she has nothing left, has little hope and mostly feels there is no future and she longs for the happy oblivion of before. Most every day life is about just getting through the day. A day that is normal to everyone else, but a struggle for Cara. Getting through a day is an enormous achievement sometimes.

We met seven years ago in a psychiatric clinic. Both of us patients. I decided to avoid her at first, because I was a psychiatric patient and I could do anything I wanted! We are firm friends now, I think, but neither of us has the self-confidence to believe it and we're too paranoid to dare. Nevertheless we know that we understand each other's miserable suffering and we understand the magnitude of each other's achievements however small they appear to be in the real world.

During periods of wellness, if we happen to coincide, we are like any other. We're positive, fun, responsible, dynamic and during these periods we cope and function, get on top of things. We don't harp on about depression and illness. When we are well we are well, full stop. Sometimes when you are well, you really, honestly believe you are better, cured and if the brain is functioning normally, efficiently, all programmes successfully installed, you are cured, for now.

## Sandy Knox

If Cara is well when I am low, I tend to avoid her. I feel alone again with the illness, no ally now that she is well. We rarely see each other anyway, even when I lived close by. If we arrange, say, four get-togethers a year we cancel three of them – it's just the way it is, the way it has to be. Our friendship relies on bouts of communication. Sometimes we're on the 'phone every day, sometimes we don't communicate for months and months.

Living with Bi-polar disorder, for me, is living two different lives for two different people. There's the me I hide away, the one with the lifeless eyes and there's the me I allow people to see. The one who seems happy and sometimes extra happy. It's hard to explain what it's like to be this way, to get across the amounts of energy and self-discipline required just to function. I'd like to give an example, I was feeling really well and confident this day and decided to make the most of it by going to the supermarket. As I entered the store I met an ex-colleague whom I was genuinely pleased to see and we stood and chatted and laughed for nearly forty minutes. By the time I was half way round the shop my mood and with it energy levels had crashed so quickly and so low that I didn't know how I was going to make it to my car. I saw my ex-colleague again at the checkout and I had to more or less ignore her. What must she think of me?

Cara regularly fights between panic and hopelessness and frets about things over which she has no control. She physically shakes and

## Bi-Polar on Benefits

finds sleeping provides the best relief though the consequent guilt of day-time sleeping is a hard price to pay. We have the same illness but we cope and function differently. We have found our own way of getting through the day.

Cara is more positive than me. She is most likely, out of the two of us, to succeed in my opinion. She's stronger than me and handles the peaks and troughs with a dignity and confidence that allows her to slip easily between her two complicated lives, or so it seems. She would never agree with this. She thinks only the worst of herself. She feels a disgrace in front of her family. She feels worthless and useless. She worries that people will think she's lazy and that she's fabricating the whole thing, making it all up, acting. These menacing thoughts are sometimes confirmed by the actions and reactions of those around her, even those she loves.

*I'm stressed because my mood has been sinking all afternoon and with it my energy, my focus and self-discipline. I'm looking at my day's attempt at housework, which began at 8.15am. Windows half cleaned, washing still to be hung out, washing still to be brought in, cupboards emptied onto work-tops, vacuum half way up the stairs, beds stripped. Where's the day gone? How am I going to clear all this away? An hour ago I was enjoying myself, looking forward to the feeling of satisfaction when I'd finished all my jobs. What the hell happened? This isn't the real me, this is not how I am, how I used to be; organised, efficient, in control. Will I ever get it back to the way it was? Are my expectations too great? Is this as good as it gets?*

*My body feels heavier, slower now – I'm clumsy. I spill a bucket of water on the floor. I'm frustrated, agitated. My house is in turmoil, my mind is in turmoil. Depression deepens, everything darkens. Self-loathing sneaks up. How pathetic can you get?*

I have experienced many occasions when a depression would just hit me out of the blue. I'd feel a dark, menacing sense of gloom and a grey cold that, as it descended, would draw from me anything even vaguely resembling hope, like one of those terrifying, predatory Dementors. You'd be left sitting in a shell of a body, it would be physically hard to talk, to smile and harder still to concentrate because all you can think about is a safe place, be it home, a telephone box, a toilet, anywhere. Auto-pilot would kick in and, hopefully, without arousing suspicion, I'd be able to act normal and polite, whilst graciously fleeing the scene. My predator following me, like a shadow, to my safe place, salivating, waiting for my signal, waiting for me to give in, as I always do, so it can devour me.

*"Dementors are among the foulest creatures that walk this earth. They infest the darkest, filthiest places, they glory in decay and despair, they drain peace, hope and happiness out of the air around them. Even Muggles feel their presence, though they can't see them. Get too near a Dementor and every good feeling, every happy memory will be*

# Bi-Polar on Benefits

*sucked out of you. If it can, the Dementor will feed on you long enough to reduce you to something like itself… soulless and evil. You will be left with nothing but the worst experiences of your life."*

*Professor Lupin's description of Dementors, from the book 'Harry Potter and the Prisoner of Azkaban'. Copyright © J K Rowling 1999.*

The following piece was written shortly after such a depressive attack.

*I'm at work, it's a big project, lots of meetings, but I need to be at home. I don't feel very well. I'm in a sort of trance here in my head and it's scaring me. I'm watching my body move and do things and I can only watch out of these eyes.*

*It's all gone now. The noise in my head. The drone of hundreds of thoughts about printers and designers and team meetings and deadlines tuning in and out all the time. It's just me, talking to me now, in the silence. I can still see me doing things, though. I'm using a computer.*

*Christ, I'm talking. My God, I'm talking to that man. My mouth is working. Words are coming out.*

*He understands me… he's smiling. I'm having a conversation. God, I'm scared. What if I can't keep this up?*

*Get rid of him.*

*I'm telling him I've got to go home straight away. That I'm not well. That's good. Thank God. What a relief.*

*I want to go home, I need to get home. What the hell's happening to me? Hurry up.*

*No. Oh God, no his hand's on mine. Get it off. Get it off. Just tell him to fuck off. Oh Christ, someone else is coming. No, it's her. I don't know how I'm doing this. I'm talking to myself and my body's out there doing stuff, talking even, without me. How? I want to go home. I need to be alone. I want to be on my own. Oh God no. No. I might cry. I'm not coping. Don't cry, please don't cry.*

*I need to be tough. Yes, I'm fighting it. Go on, go on. Come on. Come on. You can do this. We can do this. The toilet is round that corner. Make it to there.*

*They're going. Shit no, he's coming back. Just ignore him, for Christ's sake. Go on, piss off.*

*Shit, he's off on one again, I don't believe this bloke? What the fuck's he on about now?*

*Don't wanna know, can't you just like, fuck off 'cos I'm like, dying here. I just told you I'm not well. Hello?*

*God, no, I'm feeling panicky.*

## Bi-Polar on Benefits

*Please, please just go away horrible person. Please God make him go away.*

*Oh thank God, I'm waving goodbye. I'm gonna make it, the door's right there. Please don't let anyone come round that corner, please God, please.*

## Winter vs. Summer

Winter is my favoured season because it's acceptable not to leave the house.

> Don't let winter come to an end.
> Don't let the sunshine round the bend.
> Don't let them walk right past this place, or let them see my saddest face.
> The winter darkness hides my fear, but the summer sun will cost me dear.

I'm not agoraphobic, but it's not as simple as that. My comfort zone is very small at the moment. I don't extend it much and if I do it's to specified places to do specific things - my own back garden isn't even included. Days like this can be interspersed with days when I can do anything, go anywhere and I do without hesitation – like normal people.

## Planning Hell

Planning things in advance like social gatherings or even a dental appointment is not advised, particularly if you're rapid-cycling. The more you fill your diary when well, the more people you have to let down when you're unwell. Letting people down is hard to do for anyone. And nobody likes to be let down. In the last month Cara has made plans to pay me a visit four times. Each time she has cancelled. Each time I have been disappointed, which goes to show that I was really looking forward to seeing her, a compliment for Cara. I don't think she's unreliable, I know she is. When Cara makes a promise or a date, she sticks to it. That's her nature. She's honest and decent. When Cara lets me down, that's not Cara, that's the illness. I understand and I've found a good way to cope with it, I use a pencil instead of a pen when I write our plans on my calendar and she does the same with me. Last year we met up three times and that was a miracle.

I don't like to let people down, so I don't plan anything or put myself in a position where I might plan something, like I would do in mania, which more or less rules out the 'phone. I stay home in a recluse kind of way. It works for me. However for those considering a reclusive lifestyle, you will kind of become forgotten about eventually, one of those mysterious gaps in the family tree; don't say I didn't warn you.

## Bi-Polar on Benefits

Quality of life, what's that? Not something on any NHS target lists I'm sure. I think they categorise patients as suicidal or functioning. If I can get food and drink down my neck, then I'm considered to be 'functioning'. That I might not be able to leave the house or my bed for that matter, surviving on tea and the odd snack, is neither here nor there.

## Have a Heart

As I write this, Robbie Williams, one of our national treasures and sadly, a fellow Bi-polar sufferer, is holed up in a private clinic. He's suffering, probably scared and probably wishes he was dead, who knows? It pains me to hear some of the spiteful comments made about him in the press. I think people imagine he's overdone the high-life again and checked himself in to a posh clinic to sleep it off. My take on it is that he medicates himself with caffeine and script drugs in accordance with his mindset in order to control an unbearable confusion in his head; he's simply trying to find a mood that's bearable. Who wouldn't? The seemingly cruel comments may well be aimed at Robbie's profound sense of humour and fun but in reality they will only serve to validate his own self-loathing. It only highlights, yet again, an ignorance of depression and mental illness within our society. I'm not suggesting we all tippy-toe round the depressed, I'm just pointing out that it really is cruel to subject an ill mind to negative comments, like you don't feel worthless enough. You wouldn't give an old man with a dodgy heart the shock of his life for fun, would you?


**Bi-polar on Benefits vs Bi-polar on Bolly!**

Money can't buy happiness. Money isn't everything. You don't need money to have a good time. Those were the sayings I grew up with. But times have changed. Money can buy happiness, indirectly. You do need money to have a good time. And money does seem to be everything these days.

It is a fact that people with money live happier lives than people without. There are exceptions to the rule, there are people who have very little and are wonderfully happy and then there are, for example, the mean, penny-pinching, paranoid, money-hoarding millionnaires you hear about, they can't be happy.

I'm not taking a poke at wealthy Bi-polar sufferers and I'm not stamping my feet shouting 'not fair', I am taking an opportunity to highlight the effects of being comparatively poor when you have manic depression. This has nothing to do with private health care, private medication, Caribbean hideaways, fast cars and servants; this is about the everyday stuff such as gas and electricity, groceries, a haircut, washing powder. State Benefits provide you with the means to exist, provided you are careful and thank God for it, but money is a constant worry because there isn't any. Nothing in savings. Nothing stashed away.

## Bi-Polar on Benefits

Nothing valuable enough to sell. What if the heating breaks down, what if the washing machine breaks down? What if the roof leaks? Thrift is necessary, but thrift takes organising and order and sometimes you just can't manage it, so you put your washing in the tumble drier or on the radiators and turn the heating on specially, or wash only half a load (the extravagance!). Or order groceries on line and pay the delivery charge. Or miss a dental appointment and pay the fine. Oh to wear clothes that are not cast-offs from my son, my boyfriend's sons and Cara's daughters!

Modern technology provides the manic depressive with a reason never to leave the house; there's no need to. It seems anything and everything can be delivered these days. There are many labour saving services out there that would enhance the quality of anybody's life, well or not, but particularly the life of the manic depressive. During unwell periods I could have my house cleaned and my laundry done, my garden cared for and my dogs walked. My shopping could be delivered with a newspaper, cigarettes and a fresh croissant, if I want! Perhaps the occasional take-away when I'm unable to face the cooker, try as I might. I could see a specialist CBT or NLP practitioner, have them come to my home even. I could deal with Christmas and birthdays online, no need to visit the Post Office. I could buy cosmetics, music, anything I like from anywhere in the world.

So if I were asked to make a choice between Bi-polar on Bolly or Bi-polar on Benefits, I have to say, first off, that I wouldn't want anybody's Bi-polar life, but I'd be mad (no pun intended) not to want what I haven't got because money is very powerful, it can remove triggers.

"Money is the root of all evil", I remember that saying as well; funny it's the only one that still seems pertinent today.

# Bi-Polar on Benefits

## Chapter 6: A Word with the Government

## A Purely Business Point of View

It makes sense to invest in me, as it is I'm a liability, a problem, and an even greater problem waiting to happen.

For example, suppose I can't get myself back to work. I will be facing bankruptcy within a year. I'll lose my home. Any small sum I might be left with after all is sold and debts are paid, would exempt me from claiming Benefits and quite rightly so. But, that money will run out, used up over a period of time on eating, paying the rent, prescriptions, a thirteen-year-old and when it does run out you will step in and keep me, on State Benefits, possibly for the rest of my life. I've (greatly) underestimated the potential costs to you if I were to remain on State Benefits until I'm 80.

Let us assume I'm 40 years old and I will live for another 40 years. There is rent at, let's say £600pm. If I live in that property until I'm 70 years old that equates to £216k. (Let us assume that the last 10 years of my life is spent in a care home, at say £3kpm that would equate to £360k.) Council Tax Benefits for the rented property, over 30 years at £250pm equates to £90k

I will need money to live on until I reach retirement age, in the form of Income Support, at say, £800pm (which includes a disability premium); over 20 years this equates to £192k. I would also be entitled to a Disability Living Allowance, say £250pm, which, over 40 years, equates to £120k.

At 60 years old I will be entitled to a state pension (if they still exist) at say £340pm, which, for 20 years, equates to £816k.

Prescription drugs for 40 years at roughly £1k per year, equates to £40k.

The grand total thus far is over £1.8m just to keep me alive for the rest of my life! And there are many other predictable costs like specialist care, hospital stays, additional income support, community support and so on. And if, say, only 100 people are in my situation, because I'm not the only one, then that's £180,000,000.

Compare this to my (over) estimated £90k cost to the Government to get me well and back to work.

Psychiatric Services – 100 appointments @ say £200 = £20k
Psychological Services – 30 appointments @ say £100 = £30k
Prescription Drugs £40k

It makes sense to invest in me, as I said, because if I'm back to work I'll be paying taxes. I'll have a pension, some investments and probably private health insurance (if we really are to be like America) and will pay for my own prescriptions. I'll actually be putting money into the coffers. £1.8m or £90k?

## Slipped Through the Net...If I Hear That One More Time!

All I need is some support whilst I get back on my feet in the form of stable, consistent, basic financial help and the use of three specialists from the field of mental health. I need no more than what I believe I am entitled to, having paid my taxes, etc. It makes sound financial sense to invest funds in my health and well-being.

Why do you let me fall through the net? Do you know about, not only the missed opportunity, but the money drain?

In my case it is made worse by the insensitivity of your departments who should have been supporting me. Not bombarding me with brown envelopes or ignorant telephone manners. Is it any wonder I find it hard to open my mail?

I can be pro-active during well times and have gained much understanding of my own Bi-polar disorder and, unfortunately, am acutely aware of the effects it has on a life. I legitimately want to help myself. I want to get better. I want my life back.

Which is why I'm dumb-founded at your current systems and procedures for people, like me, whose illness enforces long periods of safe isolation! Procedures that require us to use the 'phone and complete forms when we physically can't or worse, get ourselves to a Back to Work Interview at the Jobcentreplus when we're not well enough to leave the house.

**Ideally**

Ideally I'd like to see the departments of health and social security working together. The GP, by simply pressing a button, could notify all relevant departments, even the dentist (then at least he'd know why I keep missing appointments at £15 a fine), that contact with this client be made through the community team. The GP would call the shots.

Community Support Teams would have the authority to instigate any social care requirements such as income support, disability allowances, housing support if it should be necessary and they should be able to do this, again, by pressing a few buttons. And this would also indicate to certain departments that this claimant is not to be spot-checked or be visited by conspicuously suited investigators pretending to be errand boys or drafted in for a Back to Work Interview because the claimant is unwell and not yet fit for work. Only the GP could re-classify a patient as fit for work at which point the Jobcentreplus, working with community support, can come into its own. Simple as!

# Bi-Polar on Benefits

## Waste Paper Bastards

Every time I receive a letter from the DSS the envelope contains mandatory leaflets. Last week I received three letters in two days, each containing the same leaflets, six in all. Leaflets that no one ever reads. I understand that, by law, I have to be made aware of certain information and that you are legally bound to provide it.

I could wallpaper a room with the amount of identical leaflets and booklets I've been sent over the last four years and that's exactly what they are, they're wallpaper, at least that's how they would be described in the marketing world, see something for long enough and it becomes wallpaper, you stop noticing it. If you're interested, I have estimated that you could reduce your leaflet print runs by 60% easily and the environment would benefit as well.

I am assuming that you have a computerised, automated system which generates letters and envelopes and stuffs them for you. And assuming you would be allowed by law to distribute leaflets twice a year, say, then can't you tell the computer to stuff your envelopes twice a year instead of for each and every letter you generate? And if you are manually stuffing envelopes in this day and age, couldn't the letter generator flag the letters requiring inserts. Or better still, do a one-off mail-shot twice a year, end of.

# Sandy Knox

**Depression is the New Bad Back**

Fraudulent claims should be investigated independently until such time as all ailments can be detected in a science lab, which is probably only a couple of decades away, when it will be almost impossible to fake an illness, even one of the mind.

There are people who pretend to be depressed and claim all sorts of Benefits from the DSS. I'm sure you could fake it if you've got the bottle (soulless eyes might be a problem though) and the standard of medical care is so poor, no one would ever know. I know someone who knows of someone who fakes it and lives very nicely doing nothing but pleasure-seeking all day. What can I say? Except that we're not all lazy, irresponsible, anti-social parasites. Nevertheless, the brush they're tarred with tars me too and no one looks kindly on a dole waller claiming depression. Unfairly, the genuinely depressed, who find it excruciatingly hard to function and cope, are under suspicion and treated accordingly by those meant to be supportive. I'd like you to discriminate between someone like me, who is genuine and someone who is genuinely taking the piss and give each what they deserve.

You see, on the one hand I've got the Jobcentre on my back because they want me at work (they've got targets to reach), yet on the other hand the NHS can't seem to get their act together to provide the diagnosis and treatment I need. I see two options: the preferred option is to treat the illness

## Bi-Polar on Benefits

so that I can work, earn a living and pay my taxes or, for pity's sake, get the Jobcentre off my back, register me disabled and leave me the hell alone.

## Drafted and Shafted

I was summoned, by letter, to the Jobcentreplus for an interview during a severe depression, which had lasted months. I was filled with dread but managed to write, and post, them a letter explaining that I was not well enough at the present time to attend and included my GP's name and 'phone number. I told them that I would like their help in formulating my CV in the future, when I'm well enough to return to work. They replied asking for details of my reasons for not attending the appointment. This made me anxious and I worried about it. As I happened to be seeing my GP for prescription medication I told him about the Jobcentreplus interview. He is well aware of the negative effects that problems with the DSS can have on a patient. He telephoned the Jobcentreplus to confirm that I was indeed too unwell, at that time, to be considered for job placement. I felt relieved, but shortly afterwards I received another appointment, another summons to the front line. I replied in a slightly stronger vein! In between times I had been allocated a Citizens Advice Bureau Agent who telephoned them. I was there when she made the call and I could hear the man from the Jobcentre on the other end. He pressed her to get me to go to an interview and I got the feeling he was questioning the validity of my illness and though the

CAB Agent didn't disclose the conversation, I could tell by her embarrassment that he was indeed trying to weed out another parasitic depression-faker. That experience sent me to a very dark place.

Another time, they sent a man to collect some information from me. It was an appointment that was preceded on my part by anxiety and nervousness, because a stranger would be coming into my home. I was confused that they would go to the expense of sending someone who seemed senior, suited and booted just to collect a piece of paper, so I questioned him, as you do. "Surely they haven't sent you all the way over here for a piece of paper. Are you here for some other reason?" He didn't really answer my question but the main reason for his visit became apparent very quickly. He came to see if my boyfriend was living with me. To see if I am siphoning money from the taxpayers fraudulently. I was livid, but kept my cool. Does he eat with me (occasionally), does he stay over (sometimes), do I do his washing (as if), where does he live (with his children, fifty miles away)? Why ask me, why not speak to my Psychiatric Community Nurse who sees me regularly who can tell you in an instant that my circumstances have not changed, that I am not co-habiting? I was told that a full investigation may be carried out , which would be lengthy and personal, unless of course, I volunteered some information (came clean). My response to him was curt and foolhardy "If you want to investigate me, be my guest. This is a typical example of the torment I've had to endure from you

## Bi-Polar on Benefits

people over the last few years. I can't tell you how many times my benefits have been stopped, started, changed and stopped again".

I showed him the paper I'd carefully drawn up, a chronology of problems, thinking he had been sent to discuss the holes in their net again. "All I can say is, bring it on. It only strengthens my case", I concluded.

They didn't investigate me, thank God, it would have crucified me at that time, and what a waste of an investigation that would have been.

Procedures within the NHS and DSS for mentally ill patients have to be changed, have to be redesigned. But in order for that to happen, project teams would have to be set up with managers to run them. Staff trained, new forms printed, a recruitment drive and someone to manage the whole project. Actually, thinking about it, I could do it for you, after all I'm not doing anything at the moment and project management is a bit of a forte of mine! It would be perfect and there'll be no pressure of a deadline because it wouldn't be one of your priorities really, would it? Sadly, there just isn't the money to pay me to do it, or so I'm sure to be told. Unless of course you off-set it against what you'd save by helping me and others like me to get back to normal. Just a thought!

## I'm Not Being Funny, But...

Regarding psychiatrist/patient communication, there's a problem. Communication is a skill, there are courses on it. Observing a patient is something you do on a ward or through a window. I want to talk with my doctors and I want them to put their pens down and talk to me, dammit!

## Receptionists from Hell

I've never been lucky with Receptionists, anywhere. I always find them unfriendly, snooty and cold. Psychiatric Receptionists need to be especially warm and friendly and should have at least a basic understanding of mental illness. Cara being told to "start walking" sent her to a very dark place. Nice one!

Trust and confidence in your primary carers, the psychiatrist and his disjointed team (no fault of his) is a vital key to a speedier recovery. I am the proof you need, Cara is the proof you need that the current way isn't working.

## Social Experience

I'm on the bottom and I've an enormous mountain to climb if I want to get my life back together. Right now, I can't even see the mountain. It would depress anyone. The whole subject is a trigger. Then I get a letter from the Jobcentreplus, a

## Bi-Polar on Benefits

ridiculously long name by the way, telling me that my circumstances have changed and consequently my Income support benefit has been reduced by seventy pounds per week to ten pounds per week with a rise to eleven pounds in a couple of months. No explanation. I deduced that they had made a mistake (again) in calculating my Benefits in the first place and now they were correcting it. Could you not have got it right the first time? Don't you realise what you are putting me through? It's like sending a packet of fags to a lung cancer patient.

Any good your health department is doing is being trashed every time the DSS fuck things up. Take a look at my file if you can get someone to send it to you.

## Chapter 7: Headhunters Pick Us!

Did you know there's a high contingent of genius among manic depressives? Yes, apparently so.

Some bi-polars seem okay for the world to know their lives are affected by depression and/or mania and all the neuroses, obsessions, phobias, eccentricities and fixes that go with it. But for these people, I would know less about myself and manic depression. Being able to compare myself with other like-minds helped me to realise that I'm not going to go mad, and what a relief that was. For example, the documentary by Stephen Fry gave me back a little dignity. No longer am I the sufferer of manic depression; that woman who's all over you one day and ignores you the next, I have what Mr Fry has, I have a touch of the Fry's. I feel so much more socially acceptable, no, fashionable now. Thumbs up!

Famous faces have clout, so the more manic depressive celebrities who own up the better - ignorance is most often cruel.

### I Wonder

On the subject of famous sufferers, the most famous one of all is Jesus. He knew what depression and utter despair was. He endured every mental and physical pain humanly possible before death, as the Bible goes.

# Bi-Polar on Benefits

I wonder, had I listened to my Religious Education teacher at school instead of defacing the picture pages of his full-colour Bibles with hilarious speech balloons, might I have avoided going through a little bit of a Jesus experience myself. Probably.

I am ashamed, truly, about the Bible defacing, but it was really, really funny. I had to stop it though – not easy hiding hysteria from the teacher. Anyway, God has a sense of humour, else where would we have got ours?

## Hang on a Minute

Given the high genius contingent, wouldn't you think we'd be sought after, head hunted? Who wouldn't want a creative genius in their think-tank? You'd think folk would be clambering to employ us. Not likely, and who could blame them.

I'm not going to land a good job immediately, not because I'm not capable, but because my CV doesn't do me any favours. I wouldn't get an interview on the strength of it. There are many things standing in my way; age, qualifications, status, but mostly it's the last 7 years. How do I explain them? Took a career break to work on my breakdown and, by the way I haven't fully recovered. Oh, and did I mention I have Bi-polar Disorder? Also, regarding previous employment, I was fired actually, after the aforementioned breakdown, but I took legal action and won. To prospective employers I'm a nutter who'd take them to court at the drop of a hat and will more than likely use all her sick leave entitlement. Apart from that I don't think I'll have any problem getting a job.

Ideally, I need a (legal) job that I can dip in and out of, pays extremely well and allows me the luxury of working from home when I feel like it or socialise if the fancy takes me, or more truthfully, when I can. Surely there must be thousands of jobs out there like that! Supposedly there's a high proportion of manics and depressives within the entertainment industry. Acting, for example, is probably the perfect job, but not for me, I'm too shy. If anyone so much as produces a camera, I'm the first in the toilets!

No, I'll probably only be good for a job in a bakery or cleaning offices (not that there's anything wrong with that). I'll have as much money as I've got now - zero. Things will be just as tight but I'll have my dignity and a sense of pride, after all I'll be a sad, divorced, frustrated single mum with a history of mental problems who wears leggings and works in a paper hat. What's not to be proud of?

Being off work for any length of time is guilt-laden. But long-term and you start dreading. There are two concerns that hit you first, how long will my company support me and what will happen to my career, because they have already written me off. Both of these concerns are very real and have very serious effects on your entire life, obviously. The fears attached to losing your job are many - mortgage, bills, credit cards, loans, commitments,

## Bi-Polar on Benefits

family. These worries weaken further a mind having trouble finding the courage to go on in any case. You sink further.

I was pressured from all angles to get back to work. "It will do you good. It's what you need. If you don't you might lose your job." I went back to work but, unfortunately, it was too soon. Way too soon! My medication was far from right. I was prescribed Nardil to lift depression and a powerful sedative to calm my nervousness and panic called Xanax (I understand it works by depressing the central nervous system) and had been taking it for a while. I have little memory of this period. Xanax or Nardil or a combination, who knows, had awful side effects for me. Without warning I would either be blinded by a brilliant light or deafened by what sounded like a siren in my head or sometimes both together. It would last about 30 seconds. It was terrifying because I didn't know if I would pass out, or die, or what? I knew these side effects weren't right, but I couldn't seem to communicate this to my £200 an hour psychiatrist. I told him several times, but he didn't seem to hear. Why?

When I lost my job, I discovered that one of the reasons was alleged alcoholism because they had a witness (a spy, actually) to my 'bumping into things'! The non-see-through sports bottle I drank from (during a 'must drink more water' phase!) was considered likely to be concealing alcohol. There was another reason for letting me go, which was justified, I wasn't performing in my role. When I was dismissed, I left the building immediately, as is the rule. I don't know how I got home.

After a month or so, I told J (Community Mental Health Practitioner). She was livid. I remember her saying that it was irresponsible of them, given that they knew I had mental health problems, to dismiss me on the spot. "You could have walked out of the door and straight under a bus" she insisted. She was so outraged she even considered calling the press (which put the fear of God in me)! Other than J, I didn't tell anyone else for months, I couldn't, too ashamed.

I was advised to take legal action against my company on the grounds of discrimination, breach of contract, unfair dismissal, etc. I was crippled with depression, numb. At one point I had three solicitors working for me, for the work tribunal, the divorce and one to save my driving licence after I was unfairly accused of a motoring offence. The work tribunal situation was a harrowing, frightening, exhausting experience, but I wanted justice and I needed money, any money, hell I'd just lost my job. It didn't get to a tribunal, we settled out of court and, for the record, I resigned. I got some money, not a lot, but hey, every little helps! I loved my job.

Xanax, the sedative that had me bumping into things, has since been banned for use in the UK, by the NHS anyway. And, for the record, I don't drink, don't like the taste. I've been known to put sugar in wine and order tea in the pub! And as for the spy, she'll get hers!

# Bi-Polar on Benefits

## Chapter 8: Self-Help Books and the Like

The more people I have praying for me, the worse I feel. I wish everyone would just leave me alone.

If you're anything like me, you'll be dreading the self-help bit, where I tell you how I pulled myself together with pomegranate juice and a dream catcher and that life is too wonderful to waste being depressed! Spare me. It just leaves me cold and feeling more hopeless and/or pissed off than ever, unless I'm manic, in which case I'd be squeezing pomegranates right now! Much as I'd love to tell you that I've found a marvellous, new, best ever way to live, thrive and prosper with manic depression, I can't. I wish! This is not meant to be a self-help book per se, in fact, it'll probably depress you, reality tends to do that!

Some books I've come across, on the subject of depression and/or mania are autobiographical in the truest sense of the word - filled to the brim with endless, flowery descriptions. Frankly, I don't care if the sun burst from yonder mountain shooting its glistening spears through your bloody curtains, I'm way past all that now. Years of endless mood cycling have left me much too cynical for all that, and with a brain that can't remember the first sentence by the time I get to the third it would be better, and I would really prefer it, if you just got to the point. Each to their own, eh?

I wouldn't put self-help in Room 101 exactly, it's just that I've got to be in the right mood to be positive and depression isn't one of them! Also, I've been depressed for so long now that I can't remember what it's like to feel positive enough to want to search through endless up-beat, cleverly designed book covers looking for my magic cure.

**Post It Notes. Oh Please!**

So when a psychiatric specialist suggests the solution to my extreme anxiety, stress, enduring deep depression and flighty manias is post-it notes and where to buy them cheap, I'm not filled with hope. Slap 'em up to remind you to do things; "take out rubbish", "go to dentist appointment", "must do ironing", "fucking phone fucking Jobcentre". Stick 'em everywhere because if you're life's organised you're mind will be organised and you will be better! Yeah? How? How do I take the rubbish out when I'm paralysed with fear to the point of taking to my bed or so depressed I don't care? How do I push the vacuum round when I can't command my body into action? Instead these notes are stark, harsh reminders of my pathetic weakness, the proof of my inability to cope with simple, everyday responsibilities and commitments like normal people.

On your post-it notes, write positive affirmations and slap them too, on everything within your field of vision to remind you how wonderful, precious and important you are to the world, "you can do it", "you

## Bi-Polar on Benefits

are special", "you are a child of the universe". To remind me what a fucking loser I am, you mean. When you don't love but worse, when you hate yourself, you can't bear to hear anything positive about yourself, you feel embarrassed and humiliated. You are worthless, you know this. You are a waste of anyone's attention, you know this. Their pity, sympathy, even their support torments you and piles on the guilt.

**How?**

For some reason it seems to be the understanding that when you're depressed you lose your intelligence. Not so, you just lose the ability to reason with it and the desire to apply it. I know what to do to help myself I just don't know how to get myself to do it. How do I talk myself out of mind-numbing fear so that I can get out of my safe-bed? How do I talk to myself when all I get is the hand? It's not possible for me to do anything unless my mood is at a certain level, any lower and I'm paralysed, too high and I opt for the pleasures rather than the pressing matters of life. In depression I'm too scared to do the very things that would help me, like sort out the mess I'm in. In mania I'll more than likely make things worse because you have no common sense, no insight. My frame of mind has to be in the right place, you have to be capable and able to do it. I know what I have to do, but could somebody tell me how?

## Sandy Knox

When I'm feeling okay-normal and have hope and confidence, then post-its can be very useful as can a whiteboard, I hasten to add, there's nothing more satisfying than crossing off a job on a list!  But when you're really low?  Forget it, nothing helps, nothing you say helps, nothing you do helps except being allowed to shut down, just for a while, in a place where nothing exists.

But you can't, because they won't let you.  "Come on, look on the bright side, it's not that bad.  You're worrying about nothing.  Why don't you get yourself out, it'll do you good.  We all get depressed, we've just gotta get on with it".  Yes, I know, occasionally everyone gets depressed; up and down according to what's going on in your life at the time.  Some people snap themselves out of it and some people carry on as normal while riding it through.  It's normal. I know this.  And sometimes I too can snap myself out of it because sometimes it's about pet-lip stuff.  But most times I can't snap myself out of it.  I become clinically depressed, sometimes for no reason.  I'm not functioning.  It means most of my programmes have crashed, I'm shutting down and I can't help it.  I can't stop it from happening and I can't do much while it is happening.  Nevertheless I have to find a successful way to live with this problem; I have to reconstruct a life filled with coping mechanisms, avoidance strategies, emergency evacuation procedures and self-enforced seclusion.  I've got the seclusion bit sussed already!

## Bi-Polar on Benefits

You never know, my brain might stabilise itself one day, but I can't waste time dreaming like that, it's now that's the problem. The solution is, quite simply, I have to get myself and my life organised. Get it in order and automated so that I can drop out now and again, as you do with Bi-polar, thus my world won't collapse, bills will be paid etc, like it was before when I could and would appear to be functioning normally with manic depression. Then and only then will I be ready and fit enough to get back to work. But right now I'm in chaos, my mind, my life. I didn't mean to, but I've let go of the reins.

About six months ago I was in a supermarket at 2 o'clock in the morning, as you do, and I hadn't been in the store long when I became pleasurably overwhelmed by my surroundings. The aisles were colourful and bright and enticing. There was a buzz, an exciting atmosphere that caught me up. I decided to look at everything, absolutely everything, as you do, and I couldn't wait to stumble upon the seasonal aisle tucked away randomly somewhere in the store. Not to mention the offers on the ends of each aisle. As I entered one of my favourite aisles, stationery, I thought about buying some equipment to help me get organised. Anything, pens, a clipboard, notepads, a filing tray and storage boxes maybe even some new files - all matching so it looks like I'm really organised and in control which, of course, I would be. I could justify the spend, because buying this stuff would give me a boost, a much needed boost, which would motivate me into getting on top of my paperwork once and for all, get a proper system in place again. This would take a weight off my mind; I'd feel more together, more in control. These would be good feelings. A positive outcome with long-term benefits for £40, it makes sense, you see sometimes little things make big changes.

I came across a magnetic white-board, this pleased me. But best of all it had printed onto it a day planner. It would revolutionise the way I organise myself on a daily basis. I hummed and h'aahed over the price, wrestling with my conscience, £7.99 plus all the other stuff was a big manic spend given my financial situation, but I bought it anyway. I decided to skip the rest of the store, I wanted to start getting organised straight away, even if it was nearly four o'clock in the morning. Driving home in the car I didn't feel great. I felt flat. Worse than flat, I felt sick as I played back the clip in my head of me, bouncing round the supermarket, eyes like saucers comparing and considering hundreds of products, ideas skimming through my head, good ideas, brilliant ideas, the kind of ideas you can make money from. I felt sick that I'd spent £53 because I didn't have £53. But my Visa did. What was I thinking? By the time I got home I was inside the grey cloud, deep. My body felt heavy, I could barely get myself from the car to the front door. I went straight to bed, I couldn't even take off my coat, and lay in shame until I fell asleep.

> *I seek sanctuary in my unconscious mind*
> *and leave my waking life behind,*
> *to hide inside the nothingness of whatever I may find.*

## Bi-Polar on Benefits

I slid the white board, day planner thing down behind some books, face to the wall, in my dining room where it gathered dust for about six months, until now. Today I mounted it to the wall, in the kitchen, next to my calendar and I've written on it what I'd like to achieve for each day, like laundry, de-poo garden, sort paperwork, nothing to write home about that's for sure! I think it's going to give me some direction. I just hope I can maintain it for a decent period of time, because, in essence, the idea's good.

## Controlling

You can exercise control over manic depression, it is possible. I do it all the time. It is a skill, which means it has to be learned. First lesson is about getting to know yourself so that you can recognise your symptoms. You have to learn to ground yourself at normal, keep yourself together at the core, this is your template. You can identify symptoms of mania and depression against what you know is normal for you. Of course, this skill is not easy to master, took me years, and it doesn't always work. When it works you are able to reason with your symptoms, present a strong case and win the battle. Spending fifty-three quid on stationery was a silly spend considering I haven't any money, but it was a controlled spend. Had I not battled with myself, who knows, I may have bought a whole office, desk, chair, the lot. I actually did very well.

**Chore Reward**

Occasionally, when I'm feeling pretty level, I can resume what I can only describe as a chore reward system. I've used it all my life pre-breakdown. It's a discipline and its basis is delayed gratification. For example, if I get a letter, a proper letter, like through the letterbox, from my favourite cousin, I will use the excitement of opening it to motivate me into doing something I don't want, or can't be arsed to do. Of course, what I really want to do is rip the letter open before it has hit the mat! Instead I assign myself a list of chores, prop the letter against a plant pot where I can see it and complete my chores before opening it, that's the deal. Then I'll calmly and maturely make a cup of tea, light a fag and open the letter.

Life's just one long weekend for me and I'm probably despised for it. Normal people are at work now looking forward to their well-earned weekend. I remember that. I don't look forward to anything now. Everything I face, I face with dread. When I'm very depressed I don't have any hope. 'Hope' programme fails to install despite pushing 'retry' all day. Hope is a pretty major programme that affects other programmes like confidence, drive, focus. But, of course, the way I'm feeling inside isn't necessarily what you're seeing. You see what I allow you to see, what is apparent to you. My calmness is because I'm shutting down. I'm quiet because I can't speak the nonsense in my head. If I'm shaky I'll just tell you I'm cold and I might seem

## Bi-Polar on Benefits

a little jumpy because I'm feeling unsafe. I might seem lethargic and lazy because I'm exhausted.

### When's Not a Good Time?

Get into a routine, get a good night's sleep and never go to bed after midnight. Not always possible, I'm afraid. Simply put, if I'm in the mood, at three o'clock in the morning to deal with my mail or my finances or the mountain of ironing, I'm going to do it because if I don't do it then, it may not get done for weeks. This could be catastrophic if there's something urgent in one of those brown envelopes such as the Jobcentreplus telling me, five months after the fact, that they've stopped all Benefits, because apparently, my circumstances have changed!

Try not to sleep during the day or you will screw up your body clock and so your sleep pattern. There are times when you just have to fall to the floor in a numb heap, unable to move, but you can't do that without attracting attention so you take to your bed. Sometimes sleep can work a little magic and you feel the better for it, but often sleep is the only break from the fear and the confusion. And even if sleep doesn't help lift a depression there's always some relief to be had in knowing you can cross off a couple of hours on your calendar, if you're lucky.

Of course, sleep has its down sides, I hasten to add. For example, there are the night sweats - waking up night after night soaking wet and freezing cold. It is unbearable. Then there are the terrifying, paralysing, nightmares. Are there words to truly describe a nightmare? And if I have sweats and nightmares together I wake-up looking like a bloodhound with a curly perm, not a pretty sight and frankly depressing in itself!

**Eat and Be Merry**

Eat properly. A depressed brain needs a balanced diet, rich in fruits and vegetables, nuts and grains, oily fish and lots of water. Stop right there! Firstly, I don't have an appetite and my chew programme won't load. Secondly, I can't think what to eat. Thirdly, I haven't got the wherewithal to put it together and lastly, I can't always get to the kind of shops that sell all this stuff, if I could afford it, because I'm depressed.

When I was growing up (in the 60s and 70s) I genuinely believed that my country cared about my welfare. That the doctors and dentists cared, even the nitty nurse cared. I still believed that when I found myself sitting in the corner of an NHS hospital on a locked psychiatric ward. But the nurses never seemed to leave their locked station, except if they really had to or to examine the slop we were going to be fed that day. They'd actually poke at it in front of us. So much for good nutrition being conducive to good mental health.

*"Research carried out by the Food and Mood Project, supported by the mental health Charity,*

## Bi-Polar on Benefits

*Mind, has shown that a change of diet can significantly improve a person's mental health. This can include reducing the likelihood of panic attacks, Mood swings and anxiety or depression."*

*Taken from the NHS Direct Website's Common Health Questions, under What Foods Can Improve My mood and Brainpower.*

Sometimes I eat because it stops my stomach from rumbling which annoys me as it interrupts the silence. Because I have no appetite, I will choose the fastest food like raisins, milk, toast, cereal. I nag myself to make porridge whenever I can because I know that the slow release complex carbohydrates will help to regulate my blood sugar, which can positively affect mood. The B vitamins, which help with the absorption of iron, are vital for a well functioning nervous system. I know this. I know what's good for me, but when you've shut down it all means jack-shit! What do you do?

### Vitamins and Minerals

I know, like most, that a poor diet can cause the symptoms of depression. It makes sense, the brain is an organ that requires a specific diet like any other organ. If the diet is disrupted then things can go wrong, like losing your sharpness and concentration or becoming low and listless. I know that I have a predominantly unhealthy diet, I survive for long periods on sugar from copious amounts of tea and sweets. I know that if I eat a healthy, balanced diet supplemented with Omega 3 and B Vitamins I would probably feel better during stable periods, which might last longer and hopefully ease the depressions a little. But, you can't eat, don't eat, won't eat the things you know you should. You can't. You don't know how. And, in any case, the required high dose of Omega 3, for example, is costly and not within my budget. During well periods and manic periods I've embarked on many a healthy eating programme, I still have the out-of-date potions, pills, lotions and gadgets in my cupboards to prove it!

What is it the experts tell us about good nutrition?

*"Not getting enough vitamins, minerals and essential fatty acids (Omega 3 oils) in your diet can have an effect on your mood too. Try to eat more oily fish, such as salmon, sardines and mackerel, which are high in Omega 3 fatty acids and also help the brain function more efficiently."*

*Taken from the NHS Direct Website's Common Health Questions, under What Foods Can Improve My mood and Brainpower.*

### Are Vegetarians Immune to Mood Disorders?

Of course not, but you'd think so judging by the above shopping list. Anyway, Flax seeds and Flax seed oil are full of Omega 3, but you probably know that!

# Bi-Polar on Benefits

## Your Help

If you're a bit of an old hand at all of this then I'm sure you'll agree that the layman's advice is painstaking to hear. Like this good idea: swap the Consultant's prescribed medication for St John's Wort, because it worked for Betty's daughter when her cat died. You want to say to them "I've got a good idea, why don't you fuck off".

I don't really want to talk about remedies, I don't really want to talk about manic depression either, or illness. I'd rather it wasn't brought up, unless you specifically hear me saying "it might be a long shot, but you wouldn't happen to know of some ingenious, yet-to-be-discovered, miracle cure I could get at my corner shop, would you, by any chance?".

## Miracle Cure

Smiling. Did you know that smiling releases happy chemicals in the brain? Yes, so smile. Make yourself smile. Smile at yourself. Smile at the dog. Smile at the wondrous beauty of nature. Smile because you're alive. Smile even when there is nothing to smile about and you will feel on top of the world.

Are you taking the piss?

## A Problem Aired is a Problem in Itself

Another self-help option is the group meeting. You get a bunch of depressives in a room for an afternoon, all strangers to each other, sit them in a circle and ask each one to address the room with a short 'bio', ie divulge otherwise private and personal information to strangers. Who wants to sit with a bunch of Me's all afternoon? It's depressing. Golden rule of being successful, remember, 'hang around successful people', so then, the golden rule of being depressed is to hang around depressed people: am I wrong? Of course, I can't hang around with successful people, not yet anyway, I'd be overwhelmed with inferiority!

There's politics involved too. You sit there critiquing the others' stories, placing them on an imaginary scale, none of them coming close to what you've been through, of course. There's also a pecking order, so to speak. The one with the worst story seems to be the greater respected for it, particularly if it involves actual scars. And those who seem to be using their illness as a comfort blanket are frowned upon.

Lots of people enjoy group therapies, the enthusiasts among us, and have gained much in esteem, self and social confidence. I think that's fantastic, but group therapy isn't, I believe, good for me. Cara feels the same.

My experience of being in amongst a lot of people with a depressive illness is one of fear and bad

## Bi-Polar on Benefits

feeling. You classify them by illness and severity. Everyone seems suspicious of the other. Working each other out. Are they manic or depressed? You have to work swiftly to know who to avoid. It's mentally exhausting. You learn quickly to avoid the overly manic (you can't always believe what they're saying, so their conversation is often pointless and tedious) which has you fraught with anxiety and guilt for avoiding someone who is probably as scared and as sad and as lonely as you are. Nevertheless you carry on regardless and compare yourself to others, envying, coveting even, the stability and apparent happiness of the seemingly recovered. Lucky bastards! So you avoid everyone.

## A Day at the Conference

*One of the main reasons I avoid people is because they invariably trigger mania. A mania that might transform me into a know-everything dynamo, or so I perceive. I went to the Manic Depression Conference in London yesterday. It was the first time in my life I'd been in the company of so many Bi-polars. Couldn't move for them. I went with Cara because she invited me. She's doing research for her next book.*

*Going there was a big deal. We were both unwell and attending this conference, fraught with fear and worry, was like stepping into an abyss. We discussed the procedure for evacuation if one or both showed signs of an unmanageable depression or mania which was likely. Cara has been fighting daily cycling for weeks. Powerful surges of energy and frantic behaviours or panicky, menacing lows dulled only for a few short hours with palm-loads of medications. And me, I've been depressed and hopeless for weeks on end, with only the respite of a couple of afternoons and the odd night of mania. The likelihood of Cara or me becoming manic before or at this conference was great.*

*We got ourselves to King's College without any of the expected problems such as parking, public transport, etc. I had travelled from West Sussex the night before to stay with her in Hertfordshire so that we could travel together. The alternative would have been to meet up in London at a specified place and time but neither of us felt up to the challenge. Cara had had only a couple of hours sleep and been up since 4.30am. She was exhausted, but hid it well. You'd never have known. I had slept dreaming about being awake, so I wasn't sure if I had slept at all. Therefore, I spent the journey not being sure if anything around me was real. Was I really sitting on a train bound for London with Cara? Yesterday I was in bed! But there we were in our separate stupours, Cara offering me Diazepam like it was a mint, I declined!*

*After trying to register ourselves for the conference on medieval textiles and pissing-off the gentleman who had to cross-out our names on his otherwise faultless page, and after finding the right building and dithering, literally, round and round in the foyer, and a couple of trips to the bus stop for a fag later,*

## Bi-Polar on Benefits

*we marched into the conference which, unbeknown to us, was in full swing.*

*It wasn't long at all before I was enthralled with the Professor's talk on the genetics of Bi-polar. The whole thing, the auditorium, the sound system, the PowerPoints reminded me of the Christmas Lectures! It was exciting. I listened and he talked about the problem genes and hereditary Bi-polar, pointing at the graphics, symbols and big words with this funky laser pointer. Now, despite having missed half of the talk, I quickly began to fantasise that I had grasped an understanding of genetic science. For example, I understood everything the lecturer talked about, all about Disc 1, its behaviours and the make-up of one's genetic code. In fact, probably understood this science far more than anyone else in the room. I would become a professor; I'd be an expert in my field. I'd be on the telly and everything. The fantasising went on and on and with it an increasing buzz of excitement. I became restless in my seat. I knew I was in danger of becoming embarrassingly manic which I feared more than anything.*

*Cara looked cool and seemed to be listening attentively. She looked great with her hot pink leather, bought for the occasion, briefcase and matching eye shadow. She looked the part, I didn't. She had a briefcase, I didn't. So I sat there for a while in my tooth-checked mini skirt and leather boots with my handbag feeling shit, lousy, shallow, vacuous, but the feelings didn't bother me for long, not once I got in front of the flip-chart with "the marker pen of power". I was beginning to display mania. I said a few funny things but nobody really laughed so naturally I assumed there was something wrong with them. I looked around the auditorium and saw a sea of grey, serious faces in drab colours and, by contrast, the bright colours of the manics bobbing about here and there. I didn't feel that I fitted in. I thought that I wasn't like them and Cara wasn't like them. And I certainly didn't want to be associated with these weird people. I discussed this with Cara at the bus stop, over a fag, and we agreed; everyone there, bar a handful, was a weirdo Bi-polar and we were definitely more your cool, executive Bi-polar.*

*Lunch was a disaster. I was nabbed by a weirdo Bi-polar claiming to be a doctor and very recently cured of Bi-polar owing to a book and a message from God, who invited himself to our lunch table and told me a joke about a vagina! Cara, meanwhile, stole herself away to the drinks machine leaving me with the 'chosen one' returning just at the punch line of the aforementioned joke which contained the offending word! She couldn't believe what she had heard and stood open-mouthed. I didn't get to eat a proper lunch, we spent most of the time hiding from him at the bus stop, smoking and drinking tea from china cups, drawing stares and glances from drivers and passengers!*

*The journey home was smooth apart from a couple of incidents which humiliated us and brought us back down to earth. Firstly, Cara accidentally flashed her boobs in Liverpool Street Station to a*

## Bi-Polar on Benefits

*stunned young man who happened to be walking towards us and who then tried and successfully cadged a cigarette from me; and then me flashing my crotch on the train to a row of people as I stood up owing to my cool, trendy necklace hooking itself to the bottom of my skirt. When we got to Cara's house she was cold to the bone, exhausted and as confused as me about the day we had just experienced. We both know that the day had actually happened but we hadn't necessarily really been there. Nevertheless we basked in the glory of having achieved what we had achieved. We had got it together and pulled it off. We actually met up and did something. I think it's my greatest achievement this year. I am proud of myself. My boyfriend is proud of me and my son is happy for me.*

*But today, I am at home and safe. No one around but my son, no one around to see me, judge me and trigger an anxious mania. It feels nice. All is peaceful. I think of yesterday as if it were a dream. I analyse my behaviour and realise that if anyone's the weirdo Bi-polar, it's me.*

### Positive Thinking and Negative Results

I don't think all this success-building, mind-bending positive mental attitude stuff is right for manic depressives. For example, "I am worthy. I am a good person. I am successful. God loves me unconditionally". There's nothing wrong with any of those as positive mantras, in the right context, but not advisable for the depressed or manic (particularly not the manic!). Take Me. Depressed Me hears negative. I know I'm supposed to be focused and driven, thinking happy things, but I can't and I feel anything but worthy. I feel anything but good and worthy, which is why am I sitting here in the dark.

But supposing I'm manic this day. I feel wonderful, it's a beautiful day, colours brighter, more vivid, birds belting out their riffs, glad to be alive, and, and, and! Everywhere I see positive messages. Church posters, bill-boards, magazine covers, shop windows, "Live life to the full. Think rich. Aim high. God loves YOU. You're worth it. Live each day like it's your last". Shit, in that case I'll book a fantabulous Caribbean holiday for me and the boys, Necker perhaps, 'cos you have to live life to the full and treasure every minute with your loved ones. They're worth it, I'm worth it. (I could invite all my family and friends, fly them out... maybe not.) I can fund it from the business I'm starting up – similar to, but much better than the one before. It can't fail, I believe in myself. Money? All in hand. Gotta go, gotta get some, you know, holiday shopping!

I didn't organise a Caribbean bash, thankfully and the shopping remained in bags at the back of a rarely used wardrobe for many, guilt-ridden weeks and was subsequently forgotten about. However, during a happy mindset a couple of weeks later I found them again – it was like Christmas (but with guilt)!

# Bi-Polar on Benefits

## Receptions

Also known as waiting rooms. When I'm depressed and sitting in my psychiatrist's waiting room the last thing I need to see is an array of 'women's' magazines. An audience of dolled-up sirens staring at me, comparing themselves to me. And what they say, 'be an amazing mum', 'do you know what really turns him on' 'read why Jennifer Aniston has the perfect life', 'feeling depressed – try mind over matter'. I feel worse. I can't live up to that.

Alternatively, I could select one of the many leaflets, some of them collectable now, on depression, alzheimer's, alcoholism, manic depression, schizophrenia, psychosis, Benefits. Or gaze at the A4 fliers slapped on every wall on group meetings, support groups, fellowships, coffee mornings.

Made even worse if you have to listen to an upbeat local radio station piped into the room as in mine!

Of course, if I'm on the manic side then the magazines and music are wonderful because they fuel excitement. The music lifts my heart and the magazines provide lots of buying ideas. I read and gaze and study and covet and pray the psychiatrist is running late!

I assume therefore that the waiting room sorry, reception was designed for normal people. The well. The stabilised. The ones who wouldn't mind if it was a bit less 'jolly'.

Same with hospitals: a couple of sofas and a new paint job does not a nicer psychiatric ward make.

## Losing One's Grip

I complain to myself or Cara, that I don't feel whole. I feel disjointed. Like I'm losing my grip on reality. Cara feels the same. Thank God, I thought it was just me. I do not feel centred at the core, as if elements of my personality have strayed into the depressed and the manic me. Therefore, I can't trust my intuition. I am frightened to make decisions.

## Music

At thirteen I was seriously into music, particularly Led Zeppelin. I know every beat, every word, well what I can make out! Music was my escape, when I could be myself, by myself.

I learned from the likes of Led Zeppelin, Jethro Tull, Kate Bush, Joan Baez, Judie Tzuke. I learned about life and love. I guess everyone is in some way affected by music and lyrics and I'm so glad I was influenced by some of the greats instead of, say, Swingle Two! There are many artists in my Favourites from all genres that sit alongside those mentioned (with Zeppelin on a bit of a pedestal) who've helped me make sense of some things in my life, as all good writers do. Most recently, I

## Bi-Polar on Benefits

have to thank Marshall Mathers whose lyrical skills helped me 'hoy-up' my anger once and for all!

**Best Friends**

You learn to avoid people really. Just in case they say something that might floor you. Like this awful woman in my village who hates everyone who doesn't earn their living and doesn't mind telling you. I avoid her like the plague! Or Cara's neighbour who has asked her not to smoke in the garden because it wafts into her kitchen window: I think they're still on Christmas Card terms! Or the unexpected 'phone call from someone I haven't spoken to in years who casually asks if I'm back to work yet, but who might as well have just hoofed me in the stomach.

It's my dogs who offer the best comfort. Loyal and loving, no matter what mood I'm in. They have got me through some tough times and take the edge off loneliness.

I've managed to drag myself on dog-walks in very depressed states (though when I am really depressed I just wouldn't be able to go). Big coat, baseball cap, tears, head down, hankies in pocket. I'm not majorly worried about meeting anyone because, hey, I'm a recluse and I don't really know anyone here. Perfect, I love it! I don't really enjoy these dog walks very often, but it's one of those responsibilities that my sub-conscious has committed to therefore one that I must do regardless. Nevertheless I'll return feeling a little better in myself, if I'm lucky, for simply having walked the dogs. And it's one more job to cross off the list.

# Bi-Polar on Benefits

## Chapter 9: Relationships

I read somewhere that manic depressives tend to get bored easily and that this is also true in relationships. Well my track record certainly stands testimony to that. I'm old enough to have enough of a history to uncover a pattern.

I love very deeply and full on. I idolise and submit and in return I am worshipped and I am so used to being worshipped now that I expect nothing less; in the same way as a neglected woman expects nothing more. But it seems that after a couple of years I become bored and, a year or so later, restless. Then someone will catch my eye, I'll fall in love and reel him in until he worships me, and off it goes again. At the time, I believe I'm doing the right thing, because I believe I have found someone whom I love and my intentions are honourable and I am loyal.

It can't be easy living with me. I get awful sad-like moods that I can't explain and try really hard to hide. They make me quiet or sometimes tearful and panicky, I hide away in the bathroom or, if I'm lucky, in my bed until it goes away. If it's not too bad I make myself walk the dogs and once or twice the cloud has retreated, at least enough for me to go home and try to act normal until bed time when I can manually switch it all off for a while, hopefully. The atmosphere in my home can be cold, flat, ominous when I'm unwell, I feel it, but on good days the atmosphere is warm and bright and alive with music and I'm happy and talkative.

There's this woman I saw on the telly who seems to live successfully with manic depression. She works from home doing something creative and artistic. Her husband can sense early signs of mania and identify stress causing triggers and steps in to help her relax and slow down, taking her for walks in the countryside, for example. Wow!

When I'm down sometimes, I become childlike in that I think the world is too big, too scary and full of grown-ups. This is when I just want my boyfriend to hold me and tell me everything is going to be all right. I want to be shrunken to fit in his pocket where it is safe. Of course, I'm not a child, so I resist the temptation to be needy, it's so undignified. But inside I'm struggling. My head feels clouded, numbed and unresponsive. Colours and sounds dulled. Doom fuelled adrenaline coursing through my veins.

On a bad day, for example, I would hear people walking past my house and dread them knocking on my door. I'd stand motionless, back to the wall, curtains closed. Not washed, not properly dressed, hair a mess. Silent, in case I'm heard and give myself away. The next day I could be a bit manic, and after hearing people outside I rush to cut my front hedge in the hope that I can nab one of them for a chat, hey, maybe even a cup of tea. I will have spent time on my make-up, hair and outfit, because I feel marvellous and I want to share my

## Bi-Polar on Benefits

marvellousness with all, because they deserve it. I imagine my house as a drop-in centre for all the lonely people in my village, everyone would know me and my door would always be open for a cup of tea and a warm, friendly chat. I'd be so popular and so important they'd say special prayers for me at Christmas!

You get the picture here, the chalk and cheese behaviour? One minute I'm sociable, friendly, over-friendly maybe. The next, I'm ignoring your calls. I love me, I hate me. What kind of person is that? What kind of friend is that? What kind of relationship could I have with anyone? From an onlooker's perspective, I'd say I seem a bit odd. A woman who is smiley, happy and friendly one day; baseball cap, head down will ignore you the next. A woman who giggles and flirts her way through traffic jams to a woman who thinks she can drive like Clarkson in a "you could get a bus through there, you tosser" kind of way. A woman who, leathered up, rides her bike through the hills, yet that morning couldn't leave the safety of her bed. A woman standing at the school gate, hood up, crying yet the next day is bright and happy and helping at the coffee morning. It makes no sense.

A loving relationship with a life-partner has got to be the most wonderful thing, if you can get it. About five years ago I decided that I would be single for the rest of my life. Not celibate, just single. I had concluded from various life experiences that relationships are not something I'm very good at. I find it difficult to hide my mood swings and they find it difficult to cope with my trying to hide my mood swings. It makes sense to live alone and it's so much easier.

**Isn't It Always the Way?**

A couple of years after making the 'stay single' decision I met someone. He put a different slant on things. Whilst he openly adores me he has not fallen at my feet! Uh? He knows the difference between depressed, normal and manic me and recognises them before I do. When I'm depressed he supports me quietly. He doesn't pressure me to do anything. He doesn't pressure me to talk to him. He just lets me be. When I'm normal, well, we are just normal. When I'm manic I amuse him, apparently, with my 'bollocks' and 'stupid' ideas and in particular my attempts at manipulating him. As with all manics I rely on my skills in manipulating, persuading and negotiating, but with him I am ineffective, therefore harmless. Result, I respect him because he tells me where to get off and he tells me we will be together forever, that there will be no 'few-years cut off' rubbish. He's in control. That's all I needed to hear!

**Some Help Hurts to Hear**

*"If you have bipolar disorder, the help and support of your family and friends can be invaluable. If they know that you have the condition and understand what it is about, they will be able to recognise when*

## Bi-Polar on Benefits

*your behaviour is out of character and encourage you to get help. They will also be able to talk to you about your illness and provide you with comfort and support when you are having an episode of mania or depression."*

*Taken from NHS Direct Website's Health Enyclopaedia under Bipolar Disorder.*

Not in my experience, sadly. It takes a lot of strength to be with people, however closely related and I strongly doubt that there are many of us with that strength. Isolation, reclusion, exclusion whatever you want to call it is par for the course, I'm afraid.

I have no regrets though a few 'I wish I had nots'. I adopted that policy many years ago. To me, if you regret something it means you knew it was wrong but you still did it. I don't believe I intentionally do anything wrong, so what's to regret? I was doing what I thought was right at the time and I believe I have a very good sense of what's right and wrong and would circumnavigate the planet in order to avoid hurting anyone, depressed or manic. Of course, I can't always vouch for my sense of logic when I'm manic or my mind's computation skills when I'm depressed and like most I've hurt some feelings along the way, but I'm not going to beat myself up about it now, I've got enough going on. And anyway, sooner or later the shame I'll feel for those I've hurt will come round again, as it always does, but not right now.

## Chapter 10: What Next?

I have no idea. I live one day at a time. There is only today, yesterday doesn't matter and tomorrow is definitely on the cards. That's all I know. That's how it is.

The day is split up. Sometimes I'll wake with positive energy and ideas and I crack on. I might completely clean my apparently filthy house, attack the paperwork or dress up and go shopping, but by the afternoon a dark cloud may have descended, in which case I'll probably be exhausted, confused, tearful and need the quiet safety of my bedroom. I'll feel foolish about my happy morning. Hell, four hours ago I was trotting up to the checkout with a trolley full of happy things, feeling gorgeous and fabulous – look at me now? And so it goes on.

Although those up-days are exhausting I depend on them to keep my head above water. If it wasn't for the manias nothing would get done and it's a welcome and often entertaining break from the monotonous blur of depression.

I may not be able to open my mail for weeks, months sometimes and it causes problems that only I will be able to sort. The pile of unopened mail grows and with it the fear of what hides within it; there will be something nasty, guaranteed. An up or well period, especially if it lasts a few days, allows me to achieve much and the relief of, say, dealing with all my mail really does work wonders

## Bi-Polar on Benefits

on my self-esteem. Life feels better for not having that particular monkey on my back, albeit temporary.

In my experience there isn't much help out there and I have only the smallest hope of ever getting back on my feet. The hardest part of a breakdown is the recovery. In fact, the breakdown, the weeks I sat safe and protected in a high-back, green leatherette hospital chair, was a doddle compared to this.

### The Ingredients to Eat My Words

Dr P, who diagnosed Bi-polar, was a locum which meant that I wouldn't see him again. Typical, you get a good one and they bugger off! I was given an appointment to see the 'new one' and, as usual, was filled with apprehension, dread even, which depressed me further. What would he/she be like? Should I even bother going?

The night before the appointment I didn't sleep, I was depressed, panicky and tearful and, by the next day, as I sat in the waiting room I contemplated leaving.

Could Dr S have fobbed me off with the Bi-polar diagnosis four years earlier, after all he knew he'd never see me again (because I no longer had medical cover)? Do I have Bi-polar? I don't really care. I just want an accurate diagnosis of whatever the hell is wrong with me. If I have Bi-polar disorder then it would confirm Dr S's diagnosis, confirm my own and Cara's diagnoses and would mean that I hadn't wasted my time looking into it for all these years. With it peace of mind and a direction in which to head. Better the devil you know than the devil you don't.

When I met my new and hopefully long-term psychiatrist, Dr J, naturally I was wary, distrusting, frustrated, scared, exhausted, fragile. He asked me the usual questions and as usual I felt unsure how to answer them. He had read Dr P's notes and was open-minded about the Bi-polar diagnosis. Could this be true? He seemed, and now I know is, genuinely interested in psychiatry and excels, in my opinion, in patient communications. He genuinely smiles, even when I'm really low, which I interpret to mean he has a handle on things, he's in control, that he's winning the fight with my Bi-polar and I find that comforting. He doesn't take any crap from me and will happily answer my questions and doesn't mind if I press him on issues, in fact he seems to enjoy it.

Dr J, at that first meeting, instigated the Crisis Team, two trained practitioners who visit you at home once, twice, however many times a day is needed. They are there to check on you, to monitor and support and support they do. These caring people offer safe friendship and a beacon of hope. They are warm and understanding. Empathetic and never pushy, never tell you to buck-up and wash your face and you can call on them at any time, day or night. Dr J was taking me seriously.

I was also assigned a Community Psychiatric Nurse who visited once a week and now visits once a fortnight. D helps to keep me real, keep me grounded not least because she is coming in from out there, bringing some of the 'out there' with her, challenging me subliminally. We can chat about anything, the illness, my feelings, her experiences, the state of the planet. It is quality time and very effective. Dr J is always briefed on these visits before my next appointment. Nice.


## Since Then

It took many visits for me to trust Dr J and his team. I find it hard to trust the NHS, I've been through too much. I'm guarded now. Once bitten and all that! Now eight months on I think I trust him. He had promised me in that first meeting that he wasn't planning on leaving his post as Consultant Psychiatrist in the foreseeable future. Instant relief, hundreds to go! He is polite and professional and you can have a laugh with him! He cares about his patients and tells them to 'phone at any time and if he can't get to the 'phone he will always return calls, as he has done mine on the rare occasions I've had to call him. When I see him, he doesn't have to remind himself of me, he remembers things, even the name of my son (whom he always asks after) and my boyfriend.

I am feeling a bit better 8 months down the line, in that I seem to be stabilising. I was prescribed Lamotrigine, which is a mood stabiliser along with Zispin and Venlafaxine, which are anti-depressants. I am prescribed Seroquel, an anti-psychotic, which quells negative thoughts and aids sleep. I feel as though I can trust myself a little more. The depression is stubborn and still lingering, though less time is spent really depressed and more time just depressed, but that's okay, I'm fine with that for now. The anti-depressants Venlafaxine and Zispin are clearly working to some degree, but I suspect the required therapeutic dose of Venlafaxine for me will be beyond the maximum dose an NHS Consultant is allowed to prescribe. One, or all of the medicines are having a greater effect on my appetite than anything else and the subsequent weight gain is very depressing particularly because I have very little to wear, very little that fits.

I am also experiencing night sweating which was at first occasionally, but now it's nigh on every night. I wake several times in the night freezing cold and soaking wet and unable to move lest the quilt sucks in cold air. I am clearly restless in the night, tossing and turning, judging by the state of my hair in the morning. I have to discuss this with Dr J and I feel comfortable doing that. It will probably mean a change of medication but hey, there are lots of others to try and, like I said, I've got all the time in the world!

Just when I thought my Benefits had been sorted I received another two letters on the same day

## Bi-Polar on Benefits

regarding Income Support. Two identical letters which told me how much benefit I would receive. They bore the same date and referred to the same payment period, but the amounts were different. So I'm in the position where I don't know how much my benefit payment will be which means that I can't budget. I could 'phone them, but I have more sense!

A week later I received a form to complete entitled 'Incapacity for Work'. I am being evaluated, again, for work. The form has many pages which ask things like, can I walk, can I sit, can I reach with my arms, can I manage the stairs? Yes, yes to all. At the end of the form is a question about mental ill-health. Do you have a mental health problem, yes or no? There is an empty space available if you want to elaborate, but what are you supposed to write? What is it they want to know exactly?

Still I shouldn't grumble, and I don't much, honest. I'm so pleased to have some support and a good psychiatrist and it only took four years. Four torturous, gruelling, fucked-up, balls-aching years! I feel I am incredibly lucky (not that luck should have anything to do with it). But the others, out there suffering in silence or shaken into frustrated exhaustion with the fight to get what they need, just a bit of help and support, what about them, because I know I can't be the only one?

**Final Word**

I've heard many times that writing one's story can be a cathartic process. Frankly, writing this has been anything but cathartic, more like harrowing, draining and exhausting. It has been an emotional struggle to relive and sift through what I am able to remember searching for appropriate pieces for this book. Not least because I live in fear of the electricity cuts in my village that switch off my aged, temperamental computer which can take days and days of button pressing to fire up again (I know how it feels)! I have to e-mail my writings to myself every few hours, just in case it crashes; I've lost loads. Why does everything have to be so damn hard?

I'm so relieved to have it out of the way. Now perhaps I can work on that book I've always wanted to write.

**Update Before Going to Press (June 2010)**

Have things changed? Are they better or are they worse? The other week I was called for another 'Back to Work' interview. My heart sank and I was wracked with feelings of failure and fear and weariness. I was in the throes of a depression that had lingered for weeks without even a sign of lifting. I wanted to cry. Could I muster the mental strength to call them? I called and spoke to a woman who was less than empathetic. I explained that I wasn't well enough to get myself out of the house (let

## Bi-Polar on Benefits

alone to attend a meeting at her office) and that, though I longed to be back at work, longed to have my normal life back, I was not yet fit for work. She insisted that I attend the meeting or my Benefits would be stopped. "What is wrong with you?" she asked. I have Bi-polar, I told her, and am in a bad depression (which is worsening by the minute, I wanted to add). I asked her if she knew anything about the illness, or perhaps I could speak with a colleague who knew something about it. "No" She said "We don't need to know anything about it, we're completely separate from the NHS and you have to come in to attend this meeting or your Benefits will be stopped, and anyway," she said "Stephen Fry has Bi-polar and he works."


(There is hope, you know, there must be, otherwise I wouldn't still be here looking for it.)

www.ingramcontent.com/pod-product-compliance
Ingram Content Group UK Ltd.
Pitfield, Milton Keynes, MK11 3LW, UK
UKHW041411180426
11947UKWH00007B/65